Praise for *A Master Plan*

"There are thousands of leadership books in print, but every now and then a special one comes along. That's the case with *A Master Plan for Leaders*. Start reading it right now. It's a life-changer."

— Pat Williams
Senior Executive Vice President, Orlando Magic
Author of *Coach Wooden: the 7 Principles That Shaped His Life and Will Change Yours*

"Your calling to leadership bears heavy responsibility: guiding people through a thick forest overgrown with human complications. This can quickly devolve into a loss of direction. Native ability is helpful, but not enough. We need a guide who has been there before. Like every good trailblazer, Dr. Gilbert Peterson marked the trees that led to his own success in leadership. In *A Master Plan for Leaders*, he not only shows how to avoid dead-end trails, but unfolds the straightest path to desirable outcomes. This is a work to read before entering the forest and reread while in the middle of the maze. It's a practical guidebook."

— Dr. Ron Susek
President, Susek Evangelistic Association
Author of *Firestorm: Preventing and Overcoming Church Conflicts*

"In this book, Gil shares important insights gathered over a lifetime of leading, learning, teaching and coaching. If your goal is to be an effective leader who exemplifies and implements Christian values and principles, you'll be helped and blessed by this book. Gil's contributions to your growth as a leader are comprehensive, clear, and up to date, and I'm thankful that he has taken the time and effort to share them with us."

— J.M. Herr
Chairman, Herr's Foods

"*A Master's Plan for Leaders* is a tool that all Christian leaders need to have in their tool box. This is for the new leader that doesn't even know what tools to use to the veteran that knows they continually need to sharpen their tools again. It covers both the "do's" and "don'ts" of leadership. It is a great resource book from someone who has walked the talk. This isn't just theory – it is principles in action."

– Phil Clemens
Chairman and CEO, Clemens Family Corporation

"Dr. Peterson articulates the essence of what true Biblical leadership in any situation is to be – mainly that the leader as a person is more important than what a leader does! But he does not stop there, as he goes on to give Biblical, practical instruction to encourage the individual to know how to lead, what to do in leadership settings and how to develop others to lead effectively. This should be a very handy 'textbook,' not in just a clinical academic sense, but in a practical living manner, for all leaders who desire to know how to lead, what to do in leadership scenarios and how to purposefully develop others to lead. If you are one wishing to be a true servant leader, then this will be a book you will not just read one time and let it gather dust on your bookshelf! This will be your manual that you will refer to consistently to know how to lead better in situations you face on your path of leadership."

– Rev. Joseph Dukes
Director of Personnel, BCM International

"Dr. Gil Peterson provides valuable guidance for leaders on how to have their home in heaven and work in the world. At a time when the ethics and morals of business leaders are under the spotlight, he provides clear guidance on how to lead with integrity sourced in God yet at the same time respond to demands with flexibility and change. Dr. Peterson provides foundational leadership principles, practical business practices and people skills all suitable for aspiring or established leaders of any size business."

– Chris Fox
Director, Creating-abilities Ltd., Leeds, West Yorkshire, U.K.

"For good or bad, the leadership culture in most Christian organizations and businesses reflects the personality of the primary leader. From the opening Preface to the closing chapter of *A Master's Plan for Leaders*, Gil Peterson challenges us to lead in a way that reflects the character of God. To grasp the critical principles revealed in this book means going beyond a fish symbol on the company website or a cross on the office wall. God's plan for Christian organizations and businesses involves a radical determination to represent the image of God in every aspect of corporate life. Don't just read this book – live this book!"

– DR. JEFF GANGEL
Director of Spiritual Formation, Toccoa Falls College

"Gil's powerful primer on biblical leadership lays a foundation any leader can benefit from – whether you're just getting started, or have decades of leadership under your belt."

– TOM HARPER
Publisher of ChurchCentral.com
Author of *Leading from the Lions' Den: Leadership Principles from Every Book of the Bible*

A Master
Plan for
LEADERS

A Biblical Perspective

Dr. Gilbert A. Peterson

LEADERSHIP
PRESS

A Master Plan for Leaders: a Biblical Perspective
Dr. Gilbert A. Peterson

ISBN – 978-0-9828594-0-7

Library of Congress Control Number – 2010931884

Leadership Press
Lakeland, Florida
LeadershipPress@gmail.com

Book Design by: Daniel Crack kdbooks.ca

Attention Churches, Corporations, Universities, Colleges and Professional Organizations: Quantity discounts are available on bulk purchases of Leadership Press titles for religious, educational, business, fundraising or sales promotional use. Special books, booklets or book excerpts can also be created to fit your specific needs. For additional information, please contact: Leadership Press, P.O. Box 7354, Lakeland, FL 33807-7354
LeadershipPress@gmail.com

Printed in the United States of America

Dedication

I dedicate this book to the godly leaders in all walks of life who seek to serve the Lord by faithful living and dedicated service and to their loved ones who give constant encouragement and prayerful support.

I also dedicate this book to my wife Dolores of some 57 years and counting. She, in spite of living with multiple sclerosis since her high school days, has been my greatest encourager, gentlest critic, most patient partner, enduring friend, godly example, loving, caring and praying supporter for me and our four boys and multiple grandchildren and great grandchildren through the years. She personifies leadership in everyday living.

CONTENTS

ACKNOWLEDGEMENTS

SPECIAL thanks to former students and colleagues who have shaped and enriched my life in both personal and professional ways. Special thanks to Dr. Greg Morris and his consistent encouragement, motivational suggestions and help in bringing this project to a conclusion.

Very special recognition and appreciation goes to Mrs. Judy Heckaman who has been a friend, colleague and editor of everything I have written since she first became my assistant when I was president of Lancaster Bible College. The tasks would not have ever been completed if it were not for her typing and editing assistance. Her patient attention to detail, clarity of expression, and consistency of thought has been a blessing.

Thanks also to those business and non-profit leaders who have taught me by their example, what it means to be thoroughly Christian in a variety of contexts. My deep appreciation goes to teachers and our family and friends who patiently guided my growth and stood with me in times of learning. Highest praise is reserved for the Lord Jesus Christ for His gift of grace and eternal salvation and daily enablement to both live and serve.

PREFACE

I

N today's profit and non-profit world there is a significant need for those who claim to be believers in the Lord Jesus Christ to practice their faith in their places of work and service. This is especially true for those in leadership positions who influence both colleagues and subordinates. This book attempts to provide some foundational leadership truths that find their source in God and His revelation to mankind as set forth in the pages of the Holy Bible.

It is my conviction that all validated management and leadership principles and practices are expressions of the very nature of the God as revealed in Scripture. God has revealed Himself in what we today call planning, leading organizing, communicating and a score of other "management type" functions and activities. When these biblically based leadership and management principles are followed, leaders reflect the very nature of God. The leader's actions then are in harmony with what God has presented and our behavior is a positive testimony to His grace.

Knowing what God has said, understanding those truths as applied to daily work expectations and requirements and being consistent in following God's Word in all areas of life requires discipline and an intelligent merger of faith and works. This book is an attempt to help leaders understand the process and practice the truth.

Sometimes leaders have what has been called an "ah ha" moment where things become clear because the circumstances and settings are just right. Most times it requires diligent study, friends and mentors who have been there to help show the way. That is what a good Christian based leadership development program is designed to do. This book seeks to compliment that process by providing information and reflection opportunities in support of leadership growth and development.

Having leaders in all types of organizations come to a mature knowledge of God, as well as live and lead in positive and God honoring ways, will fulfill the biblical instruction to do everything in the name of the Lord, giving Him the praise and glory. May God bless your study and enrich your life as you live and serve.

– GIL PETERSON
Lancaster, Pennsylvania

INTRODUCTION

THERE are scores of books and training materials that focus on methods and materials for effective leading. There are fewer that explore and explain the foundational truths behind the skills and techniques that are presented. There are even fewer that begin from a distinctly Christian perspective to correlate the truths of the Bible with the practices of the business world in an attempt to provide help and instruction for genuine believers who want to be successful in the marketplace but do it in a God-honoring manner. This book, *A Master Plan for Leaders*, attempts to fill this void by giving Christian leaders in all types of organizations a reference and study guide for positive growth and professional enrichment.

Leadership is an ever expanding field of study and there are many books on management and leadership in the marketplace today and more being added weekly. When the non-profit segment of this field is added, the number becomes overwhelming. Many times students and practitioners of leadership alike have asked which of all the books available in today's market will help them integrate their faith and values into their daily pursuits. The answer is difficult because while there are numerous books and some articles that touch on this aspect of leadership, very few take a direct and deliberate approach in attempting to integrate faith and work when it comes to the world of leadership in either profit or non-profit organizations.

However, there are a growing number of Christian family businesses that openly declare their faith and core values. In their mission, vision, core value, policy and ethical statements they attempt to proclaim their underlying faith and moral commitments. The more consistent they are in the alignment of their beliefs and practices and the more open they are in the explanation of their position to employees, customers and consumers alike, the greater respect they earn in their respective industries. In the past fifty years we have seen the leaders in large earth moving machine building companies, food processing companies, construction companies, business consulting and financial advising companies step forth and declare that their companies exist to glorify God and honor Him in all they do. Because so many have been financially blessed by their commitment to serve God and man, many share their profits most generously with their employees and various community and non-profit enterprises as part of their business commitment and core belief system.

This book is an attempt to help further this God honoring type of enterprise. While health and wealth in this world are not guaranteed by God to those who faithfully follow Him, He does promise to spiritually enrich and honor those who honor Him. As the song writer penned some time ago, "This world is not my home, I'm just a passing through. My treasure is laid up somewhere beyond the blue." While our ultimate focus is on heaven, we have a responsibility to live and serve this present age with all the abilities that God has given to us. Our privilege is to honor the Lord as well as serve others for God's glory with the gifts and abilities He has given us as long as we have breath. We are admonished to give God our best in all things, time, talent, and resources. By our faithful service and godly example we glorify the Lord.

Christian leaders who seek to be all that they can be will follow the instruction in the Scriptures to, "Let the word of Christ dwell in you richly in all wisdom; teaching and admonishing one another in psalms and hymns and spiritual songs, singing with grace in your hearts to the Lord. And whatsoever you do in word or deed, do all in the name of the Lord Jesus, giving thanks to God and the Father by Him" (Colossians 3:16-17). As this truth is applied by those who believe in the Lord Jesus Christ to organizations and the daily pursuits in the workplace, great things will take place for God honors those who honor Him. This book is designed to help in that pursuit.

One quote that has helped provide me with a sharp focus is: "Your unhappiness is not someone else's fault and your happiness is not someone else's responsibility." Being accountable for our own thoughts, desires and actions is the mature response and responsible reaction. It is to this end that this book seeks to help leaders as well as those aspiring to be leaders to think and act in a biblically informed manner as to enhance their effectiveness.

CHAPTER 1

PERSONAL LEADERSHIP

THE most difficult task in any major field of endeavor continues to be finding and developing leaders. It makes no difference what type of company you have, the key to success is putting the right person in the right place doing the right thing at the right time. The more "impact players" you attract, the stronger your organization will be.

Whether you are in a business enterprise or a non-profit organization, leadership skills and the fundamental principles of leadership are very much the same. A professional leadership presenter once said that a leader is one who will take you to a place where you would not go on your own. This is because a true leader is visionary, has practical experience, is able to communicate clearly, is knowledgeable, seeks to inspire you to your highest level of achievement and cares about you and your performance.

Discovering what leadership is all about becomes the first step on an exciting adventure of growth and productivity. This book is intended to help you discover what leadership is, how to develop that quality in others and how to become the leader God intends you to be. It is designed to help you develop the potential God has placed within you.

One other thing that can help in today's world is finding and working with an experienced coach that shares your values and understands you and the field of leadership. Enjoy the journey.

Good Leadership Demands Integrity

Good leadership is in greater demand than ever before in both profit and non-profit sectors. The problem is that everyone talks about it but very few practice it in an effective and godly manner. One man that practiced leadership in a Christ-honoring way was Tom Landry, former coach of the Dallas Cowboys. Coach Landry said that being a head coach was God's plan for the fulfillment of his life. "When it's all over I don't know that I'll reflect back on how they remember me. My own purpose is to serve God in whatever capacity He wants me to serve Him. That's my only measurement."[1]

Coach Landry also said, "God gave us talent and expects us to use it. That talent can include being a very good football player like a fast running back, a talented kicker, or an aggressive lineman. As long as Christ is the center of your life and you're doing the things with your talent that are acceptable to him, it's fine. There are many outstanding Christian people in pro football."[2] That same comment is appropriate for a Christian business person, political leader or educator. God has placed His followers in strategic places worldwide. As you review biblical history you will discover that God has done this down through the ages. Whether it was Moses in the house of Pharaoh, Daniel in the court of Nebuchadnezzar, or even Nehemiah in the court of Artaxerxes, God places His people where He wants them to be. It is up to you to be God's man or woman in the place of opportunity.

There are some things we need to consider in light of this privilege

---

1 Jack Clary, *The Gamemakers* (Chicago: Follett Publishing Company, 1976) p. 87.
2 Ibid.

– and it is a privilege. We must understand what leadership is and what is requires for it to be godly and productive. A simple definition of Christian leadership is that leadership is a dynamic communication process where one person is in the position of influencing others toward specific God-directed objectives. While this is an elementary definition, we will amplify it as we move on. Let's start by looking at what makes leadership godly and productive.

A godly leader knows Jesus Christ and strives to live as His faithful follower. This is more than just accepting the Lord as Savior and being sure of your heavenly home. Being a godly leader means that you become a true disciple of the Lord through knowing His Word and obeying His commands: all of His commands, not just the ones with which you agree. It requires a commitment to live in obedience to Scripture and absorb God's Word through regular study and devotional study.

To the basic salvation experience is added another layer, which is both understanding the communication process and learning how to use it to the best of your ability. Your goal is to help others be all that God intends them to be.

Next, leaders are only leaders if they have followers. Ironically, a prerequisite of leadership is your knowing how to be a faithful follower. Only by first experiencing follower-ship will you understand what expectations followers may have of their leader, and what expectations are reasonable for you to have of your own followers.

A significant indication of one who is living in obedience to Christ is found in examining their integrity. Being godly at home, at work and at play is not optional; it is a fundamental requirement of Christian leadership. But what exactly is integrity? The Oxford-English Dictionary states that the word integrity comes from the Latin *integritas* which means wholeness, entireness, completeness. The root word is *integer* which means untouched, intact, or entire.

To further amplify the point, Dr. Warren Wiersbe asserts in *The Integrity Crisis* that integrity is to personal or corporate character what health is to the body or 20/20 vision is to the eyes. A person with integrity is not divided (that's duplicity) or merely pretending (that's hypocrisy). He or she is whole; life is "put together" and the various roles are in harmony. People with integrity have nothing to hide and nothing to fear. Their lives are open books.[3]

On the other hand, people without integrity always have something to hide. Those become deep dark secrets which haunt the leader who struggles with integrity issues. Jesus Christ took a very dim view of people who lacked integrity. In Matthew 6:19-24 He paints a picture of the two-minded man who has two outlooks on life and two masters in life. As a result he has difficulty keeping truth and error separated. In fact, a person without integrity, the Bible says, actually thinks that darkness is light (1 John 1:5-6).

A godly leader avoids the very subtle but fearsome trap of duplicity. The typical pattern starts with hypocrisy. Here a person lies to other people about their relationship with the Lord, or other significant issues. The next step is to lie to themselves and believe it. Again, it is a subtle but nasty trait that can easily become a habit. The final step downward is to actually lie to God in thought and prayer. The only way to avoid this and maintain our integrity is to walk in the light as God has instructed.

When leaders fail because of a deficiency in their integrity, others are often surprised and shocked. In fact, the leaders themselves are sometimes taken off guard and refuse to face the real issue, instead striking out against those who hold them accountable for their duplicity. In these cases, the light has become darkness for them and they can no longer discern right from wrong. Sadly, there are too many similarities between the failures of leaders in the religious world and leaders in the secular world when it comes to morality and integrity. We need leaders in all walks of life who not only profess truth but live it. The words of the mouth and the walk of the life must be consistent if truth is going to win the day. Without integrity there can be no true leadership; and without God integrity is unattainable.

---

3 Warren Wiersbe, *The Integrity Crisis* (Nashville: Oliver-Nelson Books, 1988) pp. 21-22.

Enduring Character

In examining what we would call good leadership, it is important to consider character and not just competency. There are many knowledgeable and skillful leaders who fail when it comes to issues of character. Yes, competency will make the difference between an excellent performance and a mediocre one. However, character makes the difference between enduring leadership success and ultimate failure.

God works in and on the human heart, but our hearts must be pliable and open to instruction, correction, maturing and growth. It has been my privilege to know scores of Christian leaders during my lifetime. I have observed that those whose lives were marked by prayer, openness, honesty and humility were the ones who made the most positive impression on my life and the lives of others. Some leaders were smooth in style, fluent, and personable, but lacked the authenticity that is evident when the Holy Spirit is in control. Such leaders make excuses, take shortcuts and emphasize public activities to the neglect of private growth and even private integrity. Avoid these influences in your life. (For further reference see Jeremiah 17:9, Psalm 139:23-4, Matthew 15:10-20, Proverbs 4:23.)

It is not just the source of integrity that is important; it is the integrity of the source that really counts. If the foundation for your integrity is anything other than the holiness and truthfulness of God, you are basing your life on what the Bible calls shifting sand. A man who led Christian organizations and has lived his life in an exemplary manner was Dr. Hudson T. Armerding, former president of Wheaton College in Illinois. He authored a wonderful little book entitled *The Heart of Godly Leadership*.[4] In this work President Armeding explains that it makes a difference which god we serve. Some people say as long as you have faith, that's all that counts. Some even argue that all the religions of the world are right! While this is a logical impossibility, logic never seems to bother someone whose mind is set on error.

---

4 Hudson T. Armerding, *The Heart of Godly Leadership* (Wheaton, IL: Crossway Books, 1992).

Armerding stresses that the "living God" is the true God, the only one with integrity. He is consistent, reliable, never-changing and has revealed Himself to us through the sending of Jesus Christ. Theologians use words such as omniscient (all knowing), omnipotent (all powerful) and omnipresent (present everywhere) in an attempt to capture the essence of who He is and what He does. A complete reading of the text of both the Old and New Testaments will reveal a God who is holy, just, personal, loving, forgiving and who invites everyone to repent and trust Him with their lives for time and eternity.

"God is great and God is good, and we thank Him for our food," is one of the first prayers I was taught as a child to remind me of His provision and protection during my life. The older I get the more precious that truth becomes. The integrity of God is central to the Christian faith and it is the model for us to follow in all our dealing with others; from family and friends, to customers and colleagues. It should always mark our decisions and actions.

We must maintain a clear and consistent testimony if we are to lead with authority in a trustworthy manner. Coach Tom Landry, as mentioned before, was a noteworthy example of this. His exterior manner seemed to reflect an inner calm and assurance. Others noted it as well. Jack Clary wrote that the inner serenity was genuine and connected to Landry's deep Christian faith. He quotes Landry's explanation: "I'd hate to say my faith's a rock but it's true. A lot of people say, 'Well, he's a Christian because that's the only thing he can fall back on.' That's not true. It is my strength; it gives me inner peace. Without my faith, I'd be in real bad shape. Faith gives a man hope and hope is what life is all about."[5]

Christian leaders consistently act in accordance with their moral principles and within their value system. There is a real sense in which our integrity encompasses our personal identity. It is more than consistency between personal values and conduct. Integrity as a description of character is about faithful adherence to ethical

---

5 Clary, *The Gamemakers*, pp. 86-87.

principles like honesty, respect, responsibility, fairness, and compassion. *Subscribing* to decent moral principles is not enough. **A person of integrity** *must act on decent principles – and do so consistently.* Integrity is the bridge between character and conduct.

Writing in *The Wall Street Journal*, Emory Thomas penned an article that perfectly illustrates this principle. Ernest "Bud" Miller, president and CEO of the real estate company *Arvida*, once closed regional offices, completely reorganized departments and slashed his 2600 member work force in half. By implementing these drastic measures, he turned a money-losing company into a profitable one. But despite the trimming, Miller believed one layer of fat remained. So he resigned. He said he could not justify remaining with the company. He could not look at the people whose jobs he had terminated and apply a different standard to himself. He said that every fiber in his body told him to stay but professionally, this was the decision that had to be made. The move eliminated one of two senior jobs at the company and the chief operating officer of *Arvida* became the chief executive officer. Miller, 53, gave up an "upper six-figure" salary package, but did what was right. That is what is meant by integrity. You lead by example.

Loyalty vs. Integrity

Another outstanding spokesperson on this topic is a man who was transformed by the power of God and became a model of integrity. Charles Colson, in the book *The Power of Character*, provides an insightful analysis of integrity and loyalty in a chapter entitled "Knowing What is Right is Not Enough."

One day after a lecture, Colson was questioned by a tall Marine master-sergeant: "Mr. Colson, which is more important, loyalty or integrity?" The Marine Corps is noted for their allegiance to the motto *semper fidelis* and Colson, a former Marine himself, recognized the magnitude of the question. Yet his answer was sobering: "Loyalty not attached to a cause that is moral can be the most dangerous of all virtues."

To illustrate his point Colson described his experience in the White House. When as human beings we believe that our cause is just, we are capable of infinite self-justification. Our conscience becomes not a guide, but an accomplice. Intending to do good, we end up neck-deep in compromise. He explained, "Clearly it is possible to be self-righteous without being righteous. Clearly, being a man or woman of character requires something more than intellectual commitment to noble goals and high ethical standards. It requires something more, as I discovered, than the echoes of a father's advice or even a Marine code."

Colson went on to define it more precisely. "What is this something more? It is the disposition to do what is right. It is not enough to know what is good; we must also love the good and have the will to act in accord with it. This can hardly be more urgent, given the collapse of character in American life. We see an epidemic of broken marital promises, leaving women in poverty and children in emotional chaos. We see a growing number of brutal juvenile offenders, with vacant eyes and hollow souls, who have lost all contact with mercy and morality. We see scandals in government, business and academia which have become so commonplace they have lost their power to shock. In every class and community the breakdown of character is the storm in which we are attempting to navigate."[6]

We must never mistake loyalty for integrity. It costs something to be a person of integrity when it conflicts with loyalty. You can be sure that some day in some way the question of loyalty will be raised by leaders who are insecure and insist on having followers who tell them they are right, even when it leads to costly mistakes. Some leaders only want to hear "good news" and consider anyone who differs with them to be disloyal or a threat to their power.

I once had this type of experience in my life. I was confronted by my boss and he demanded that I declare my loyalty to him. Even

6 Michael Josephson and Wes Holmes, editors, *The Power of Character: Prominent Americans Talk About Life, Family, Work, Values, and More* (New York: Jossey-Bass, 1998) pp. 294-295.

though we had spent countless hours talking business and sharing dreams as well as creating plans and activities together, there came a point where he was being criticized by many people and sought a focus for his frustration. It happened to be me. He demanded that I declare my loyalty to him before even responding to anything he had said.

Being younger, less mature and somewhat frustrated by the confrontation, I replied, "What you are asking for is stupidity, not loyalty. Loyalty is always telling you the truth. But telling you what you want to hear or simply agreeing with you when I believe you are wrong is stupidity."

We need to recognize that loyalty is being honest and truthful in our encouragement and support of friends and colleagues. While this particular event did not work out the way I would have preferred (I eventually sought other employment), I learned tremendous lessons from this experience that has helped me for the rest of my life.

This is not a license to complain or disagree for the sake of disagreeing. Some people act as if they have been given the gift of criticism! However, competent and secure leaders understand that wise decisions come only after tough and even unwanted questions have been asked and successfully answered.

Pause and Reflect

What is your reputation with God?

Some find it easy to mislead others with clever words, well designed resumes and deceptive manners. However, God knows who we are and sees all that we do. He is not fooled; He knows our thoughts and the inner motives that drive us. What does he see in your mind and soul today? In spite of what He sees, He loves us and seeks the very best for us. He has prepared a heavenly place for us and seeks our fellowship on a daily basis.

What steps are necessary for you to correct mistakes you have made? To forgive someone for the hurt they have inflicted on you? To be an encourager to those who work around you? Whatever it takes, it is worth it to become the leader God has designed you to be. While the steps may not be easy, God promises His strength when you commit to His plan.

It is essential for godly leaders to maintain a close fellowship with the Lord. Daily inspection, daily prayers for forgiveness and a persistent and consistent study of God's Word are the path of success. How is your prayer life? Do you end each day talking to the Lord about the events and happenings you have faced? Does your prayer life exhibit a concern for the things that touch the heart of God? Does your prayer life embrace the people you deal with every day as well as your friends and acquaintances around the world?

In your daily schedule, be sure to allot time for personal inspection in prayer, reading of God's Word and intercession for the people of God world-wide. The most precious hour of each day can be the time you personally "catch up" with the Lord. Over 50 years of ministry has taught me that when the prayer life falters, so does the personal life. Maintain consistency in your spiritual life.

Leadership Requires Flexibility

It is reported that someone once asked the Duke of Wellington how he defeated Napoleon. He replied, "Napoleon's plan was made in wire, but mine was made in string." Wellington recognized the value of flexibility and as a result, was successful.

Leaders have to handle the unexpected. While some are prone to rigid, uncompromising plans, others realize that planning is a continual process. That ability to flex is often the difference between a leader and a manager. Managers usually have set routines and rules by which things are governed, but leaders learn to live with an ever changing landscape.

In most organizations you find some managers who fill the role of leader and some leaders who fill the role of manager. A pure manager, when confronted with a problem outside the normal routine, is generally unsure of how to respond. A pure leader, when faced with the same situation, thrives on the challenge and generally responds with innovative and successful answers. The manager tends to rely more on accepted and approved procedures and therefore avoids risking the creative and more innovative solution. Great talent can be wasted by a lack of boldness.

Also, leaders tend to search for answers "outside the box." They are willing to experiment with new and untested approaches, relying on their innate leadership ability and instinct for solutions more than on historic patterns of activity. *Carpe diem* – "seize the day" – is their mantra.

Leadership is a complex undertaking that involves steadfast determination. With this resolve, your followers can have confidence and a secure path to follow when accompanied with thoughtful flexibility. Together, you remain alert, constantly searching for the best alternatives and appropriate solutions.

Rigid adherence to a plan coupled with an unwillingness to change has caused a myriad of leadership failures. Just ask Napoleon. Quality leadership almost always requires strategic adjustments and at times, even retreat or as the Marines put it, the need to regroup.

Finding the right balance between inflexibility and flexibility is not an easy task but a crucial one. Books that chronicle the lives of political presidents reveal that followers judge leaders to be effective who remain true to their stated convictions even if the final results are not what they expected. In a similar vein, they tend to view as ineffective leaders who vacillate and rapidly agree to change, depending on the advice of the moment. This is not an endorsement of stubbornness but reveals that consistency in purpose, manner, convictions and beliefs can keep necessary flexibility from becoming counterproductive.

When a leader considers seriously the core values and beliefs upon which they base their decisions and commits to be consistent in their decisions and behavior, their followers tend to have a great deal of confidence in them. When a leader is easily influenced by contending ideas and advice and is quickly swayed from one viewpoint to another, they are viewed not as flexible but lacking courage and thoughtful convictions. We need to make sure we major on the things that are true and enduring, while remaining relevant, open and informed about the needs of our people and our organizations. Leadership requires independent thinking and the courage of one's convictions.

Pause and Reflect

What is the difference between regrouping and retreating when facing a difficult problem? When you have charted a course and are faced with facts that do not support your direction, what do you do? What is your plan for regrouping or readjusting?

How often do you evaluate the success of your plan once it has been launched? What points along the way have you designated as success indicators or failure indicators to consider the potential success or failure of your plan so you can adjust accordingly?

Every wise leader knows that change is inevitable and that some of the changes around us will affect what we have planned. Being appropriately flexible, with ready alternatives in place, is the best way to think through our strategies and executive successful plans.

Improvement Requires Change

How do you feel about change? Try on this statement for size: "There is no improvement without change." Is it true or false?

Rooted in the definition of improvement is the concept of change. It is not to say that all change is improvement, because you can change for the worse, not the better. In fact, that is too often the case. But it is a fact that you cannot improve without changing!

I would be the first to admit that change is difficult. And I would further admit that the older I get the more resistant to change I become. But the reality is that change is inevitable. I have learned that unless we work at both accepting and directing the changes in our lives we will be victims and not victors. Further, I have realized from my leadership studies that change is increasing exponentially and the more we can learn to anticipate and manage it, the better off we will be.

This matter of change and adaptation permeates every walk of life. No industry, organization, or profession is exempt. You cannot grow unless you change; therefore all physical growth, social growth, mental growth, or even spiritual growth involves a change in life. The opposite, however, is not true; as indicated before, all change is not positive. It is important to realize that change does not always represent progress. The other side of the coin is that if we do not change there will be no progress.

Are you more a leader or a manager when it comes to facing the unexpected? This is one reason people often oppose change. I am fond of using the expression, "I love change – when I initiate it!" You see, when we are leading a particular change we have already had time to anticipate and answer objections for ourselves. We have our eyes set on a positive future goal, we are championing a cause. However, for those who are being introduced to the change, change can be scary and all change involves some losses and some pain and any departure from the norm means more adjustments!

Most leadership texts will tell you that to be a leader is to be a change agent, yet the first thing a leader must change is themselves. Every leader has to accept three truths: 1) they have changed and been changed in the past; 2) they must be willing to change as their followers are changed; and 3) they must be willing to face the problems of leading people through change. These are not easy tasks in most situations. The leader must demonstrate courage, vision, be willing to answer scores of questions and resist the negative players who challenge change just because it is change. One thing that growing leaders learn is that to be a leader you must be a learner. This is because when you are leading people and expecting them to change you must be constantly learning. The leader that stops learning will eventually stop leading.

Foundational Assumptions Regarding Change

When a leader studies change, certain basic concepts appear to be self evident. They include the following:

1. *Change is a fact of life.*
   We are born, we grow and we die. These steps are part of the changing landscape of life. Information networks, workplace patterns, styles of clothing, work and home schedules and a host of other things are always in flux.

2. *Change is best negotiated if there is a leader who is experienced at leading the group through change.*
   At home or in the workplace, wherever people are, change is always occurring.

3. *Change will be better received if the one leading change has a track record of effective leadership.*
   Where a leader has had a positive impact on the lives of those they lead, change is much more easily accepted. The one statement that best sums it up is, "I trust you."

4. *The greater the change, the more preparation must be done before implementing it.*
   People will generally resist change and need to be comforted by knowing what it entails in terms of its personal impact upon them.

5. *Change must have a logical and reasonable direction.*
   Too often change is instituted for its own sake. Sometimes it is because others are doing it. Other times it is because a new leader wants to duplicate what they had in another company. None of these are good reasons for change. As a leader you must always think in terms of what improves and enriches. What will the new innovations bring to your business? Without some increase in meaningful and long term value, the changes will probably be short-lived.

6. *Change is inevitable, whether we want it or not.*
Wise and godly leaders recognize that they must lead changes if they are to have a positive impact upon their company. When a leader refuses to consider new methods or innovations to enhance their business they will become stale. Further, as culture changes around them these leaders fail to keep pace and grow; consequently, they tend to look to the past and not to the future, from where success could come. As a result they become ineffective.

Leaders as Change Agents

Not all leaders want to be change agents. In fact, some organizations have boards of directors or another type of structure to control the amount of change within the organization. Boards are generally committed to the *status quo*, for their mandate is to oversee and maintain the mission, resources, and integrity of the business, as well as fostering and approving long range plans.

The more insecure a leader, the less likely they will be to initiate change. Tentative leaders like the comfort of the way things have been done in the past and the results that they can show for those efforts. The fear of the unknown which any change brings is a threat to stability and the leadership that is in place.

Are you an agent of change in your organization? Consider the following:

1. Organizations seem to do their best work when they encourage innovators and innovation within their teams. This is not a natural tendency. Identify, nurture and provide opportunities to team members who have the ability to be creative.
2. Leaders must be objective when presented with new ideas. Too often a valuable innovator receives a negative reaction when they first present an innovative idea and they become reluctant to share in the future.
3. Do not simply try to duplicate what others are doing. If you do you will miss the paradigm shift that is occurring in your

business. Seek new methods, new products and new approaches to what you are doing to remain on the leading edge.

4. Always know what the rate of return is on the investment of your time and resources. Effective leaders do not waste the time, talent, or resources of their company.

5. Keep your word! Maintain a reputation of integrity in all you do.

6. Surround yourself with people who are smarter than you are. Recognize that you need the combined talents of many different ways of thinking to deliver the best in products and services.

7. Possess a philosophy of life that views people as most important, change as inevitable and truth as your mandate. Never compromise on the most important things in life but demonstrate them in all you do.

8. Great leaders know how to make decisions and do so in a timely manner. Effective leaders do not act by simply following the majority. Seek consensus but never insist on it!

9. Value highly those who work with you to create positive change. Those who assist you in developing and implementing your business plan are a special blessing from God. Properly reward the right people, not the ones who you think will serve better because of the reward.

10. Maintain a vital and growing intellectual and spiritual life. Your ultimate reward is in heaven so live the life of a godly leader.

Leadership is not all only about change but change is always involved in leadership situations. As mentioned before, a teacher once observed that a leader is one who will take you to a place that you would not go on your own. He will help you achieve things that, in all likelihood, you previously would never have considered. He will engender in you a positive spirit of accomplishment that you might never experience on your own. He will coach, question, encourage, cajole, in a word, help you become better over time.

Pause and Reflect

Think about your organization. What are some of the programs or methods that have worked in the past that do not seem to be working in the present? Why are they not working? What changes can be made to make them successful?

What new programs are now being introduced that may not have long-term success? What are the principles guiding these changes and what are the methods that are indeed changing along the way?

Who are the innovators in your group? How can you encourage them to continue to surface new ways of doing things?

How do you lead change? Do your colleagues trust you enough to follow willingly? What are you doing to stay ahead of the curve?

Beyond Good to Godly Leadership

"A fiery horse with the speed of light, a cloud of dust and a hearty 'Hi-Ho, Silver!' The Lone Ranger rides again!" This is a great grabber for an old time radio program but a poor description of a leader who want to be a Christian leader. The unfortunate fact is that a large number of Christians accept this concept when they think of leadership. Leadership, they believe, is mysterious; it is bestowed on a few gifted people. The chosen one is lonely, strong on authority and control; and always a winner.

This concept of leadership, however, is quite different from what is described and illustrated in Scripture. Rather than centering on power, skills, plans and abilities, the Bible emphasizes the character of the individual and the role the person is to have in the functioning of a local body of believers. God focuses on people, establishes the character objectives and demonstrates the proper functioning roles.

God has chosen to work through people as evidenced by Adam in the Garden of Eden (Genesis 1:26-31), Abraham (Genesis 12:1-3) and Joshua (Joshua 1:1-9), up to and including this present day (Ephesians 4:1-16). People are enabled by God to help, teach, encourage, guide, admonish, love and influence others to reach their potential in both the physical and spiritual realms.

For those who are Christian leaders it is important to realize that everyone in the body of Christ has something to contribute to someone else. There is an interdependent relationship between Christians that is God-designed, purposeful and profitable to all believers. Paul makes a strong case for this in 1 Corinthians when he writes concerning spiritual gifts.

> For as the body is one, and hath many members, and all the members of that one body, being many are one body, so also is Christ. For by one Spirit, were we all baptized into one body, whether we be Jews or Greeks, whether we be bond or free; and have been all made to drink into one Spirit. For the body is not one member, but many. If the foot shall say, Because I am not the hand, I am not of the body; is it, therefore, not of the body? And if the ear shall say, Because I am not the eye, I am not of the body; is it, therefore, not of the body? If the whole body were an eye, where were the hearing? If the whole were hearing, where were the smelling? But now hath God set the members, every one of them, in the body, as it hath pleased him.
>
> – 1 Corinthians 12:12-18

Here the apostle shows that God not only works through people, but that each person has a special function to perform in their life-time. This can be extended further when we consider that everything we do "in word or deed" must be done for the honor and glory of the Lord. We cannot neatly divide our world into sacred and secular. For a true believer, all that we do – leadership included – is some type of ministry that should bring honor to God. Typing, speaking, building, writing, painting, sculpting, organizing and communi-cating are activities that affect others and we are responsible to do them to the best of our ability and for the glory of God.

If we take seriously the premise that **leadership is a dynamic** communication process where one person is in the position of influencing another toward a particular goal, then there is both a moral and spiritual dimension to leadership that must be considered. When one attempts to influence another or help someone achieve a goal, then the nature of the goal, the method of influence, the motivation behind the process all have moral and spiritual issues that need to be examined.

Pause and Reflect

In what ways have you mentored or coached someone to be what God intended for them to be? Who do you presently work with that needs counsel and encouragement from you? What particular skills as well as character and spiritual strength do you bring to bear on your work with others as you lead them?

Take time and plan to spend some time (30 to 60 minutes per week) helping someone increase their knowledge, improve their skills, or adjust their attitude so they can be a stronger and more effective leader.

A Christian View of Leadership

We have defined leadership as a dynamic communication process where one person is in the position of influencing others toward a particular objective. Let's take a closer look at what is involved in this definition. There are five key elements: 1) the leader or influencer, 2) the methods of influence, 3) the one(s) being influenced, 4) the setting in which the influence takes place, and 5) the end toward which the influence is directed.

Christian leadership, by the very fact that the word leadership has been modified, needs a more definitive statement. It is not merely adding the fact that a Christian is now the one who is doing the leading. No, a different dynamic is added to the concept which both enriches it and, in a sense, narrows it.

What is Christian Leadership?

Christian leadership is a Holy Spirit-guided dynamic communication process where a believer is in a position to both influence and help facilitate the development of others so that they can fulfill their God intended purpose. Let's look at this concept in greater depth.

The Holy Spirit

First, Christian leadership is a process guided by the Holy Spirit. While the Holy Spirit exercises general influence over all humankind, He has a series of very specific ministries to the believer. He guides us to truth (John 16:13), controls movements of believers (Acts 10:19), selects Christian leaders (Acts 13:2), gives spiritual life (John 6:63), comforts (John 15:26), convicts of sin (John 16:7, 8) and in general, leads all believers who yield to His influence (Romans 8:14). A Christian not yielding to the Holy Spirit may very well be leading in a non-Christian manner.

Communication

Next, Christian leadership is a dynamic communication process. It is dynamic in that communication is always going through some process of change. Nothing in the communication area remains static. This is true whether the communication is verbal or non-verbal. Influence, which is the essence of leadership, is exercised via the tools of communication. The word symbols that are chosen have importance. The inflections and manner of delivery affect the process. Silence can be a communication device. Gestures, facial expression and a host of other items together cause the communication process – which is the heartbeat of the leadership process – to be a dynamic and essential part of understanding leadership.

The Leader

Every person is in a position from time to time to communicate with, influence and thus lead others. If you are married, you are "in a position" to influence your partner and thus lead. This is true whether you are the husband or wife (Ephesians 5:21; Colossians 3:16, 17 ff.). If you are a parent you obviously are responsible to lead and influence your children (Deuteronomy 6:5-9; Ephesians 6:4 ff.). The Scriptures also speak of those who are teachers, those who govern and those who by faith in Christ have the responsibility to share Christ (influence, lead) with those around them.

Everyone who has personally received Christ as Lord and Savior has the privilege and responsibility to be an influencer (leader) of others in terms of Christian truth and life. While we do not all have the same personality, experience, or verbal facility, we cannot excuse ourselves because of some personality weakness or lack of opportunity.

Not everyone's leadership (influence) effectiveness will be the same. Nor will everyone's breadth or scope of leadership (influence) be the same. We are not called to be reproductions of other Christian people. We are called to be followers of Christ and to be faithful in whatever sphere of responsibility God gives us (1 Corinthians 4:2). Some will be teachers. Others will be administrators. Still others are helpers and the list can go on and on. We are all "in a position" of leadership whenever we have the privilege of being in the presence of others.

The Style

The fourth element in the Christian leadership process is the actual influencing or facilitating process. This is where the variety of roles and interpersonal relationship situations come into play. There are formal situations such as classrooms, church services and board meetings where the structure sets forth specified roles for people such as teacher, pupil, pastor, chairman and the like. There are also informal situations such as ordinary conversations, talking about a common interest or problem with others over a meal or dropping by to observe and possibly talk about a person's work or recreational performance.

It is in these settings that the style of a person's leadership is seen and evaluated. Some leaders tend toward a strong "do what I tell you" approach, while others tend toward a "let me know what you have done" approach. A person's personality, the type of work being done, the element of time, the ability of the followers as well as a host of other items come together to produce the leader's style. In addition, the intervention of the Holy Spirit of God produces a dynamic that is not measurable or easily defined.

Later, particular attention will be paid to the biblical models or pictures of leadership that add another vital element to our understanding of Christian leadership.

The Follower

The fifth part of the Christian leadership concept is the follower or the one being influenced. This could be a believer or a non-believer. This could be one person, a small group, or a very large group. If you buy into the premise that all of us are leaders, both potentially and actually, then it is also true that all of us are also followers. We are on both the giving and the receiving end of the personal influence. This element and the communication element are the two factors common in Christian and non-Christian leadership. The other four elements are distinctly modified because of God's direction and His dealing with us.

The Objective

The sixth and final part of Christian leadership is essentially twofold. First it is seeing other people develop and fulfill their God-intended purpose in every area of life. A Christian leader cannot be satisfied with only helping people become successful in this life. For the Christian leader, one key objective is helping all individuals become complete persons. If the leader's follower or followers have not trusted Christ as personal Savior, then the Christian leader will seek to share their living faith in Jesus Christ in a personal way. This being considered, the next objective is to facilitate the individual's personal and professional growth, development and productivity.

If the follower is a believer, then the primary objective is for that person to grow, develop and produce as a child of God for the glory of God and the good of others. If the follower is not a believer then a leader has the responsibility to give a good witness and be a good witness. Living out one's beliefs and helping others do the same should be a Christian leader's passion.

There is a second equally important objective and one that is tied together with the personal enrichment side of helping others. That objective is for leaders to move an organization forward and upward. A leader has the privilege and responsibility of helping organizations improve, grow, and fulfill the purpose for which they were created. It is a corporate responsibility that leaders do not take lightly. The excitement of seeing improvement and success is a special thrill for leaders.

Pause and Reflect

Write your own definition of leadership and explain it to someone else. Explain the difference between leadership and Christian leadership.

Make a list of the colleagues you know who have expressed their Christian faith in some way and seek ways in which you can encourage them and assist them in their daily work and walk for Christ.

For colleagues whose spiritual condition is uncertain, commit to pray for them daily and as the opportunity presents itself share your faith and values with them. Pray before you speak to them and anticipate what God can do. Always treat your colleagues with grace and care.

Natural and Spiritual Leadership

In his superb book, *Spiritual Leadership*, J. Oswald Sanders grapples with the distinction between natural and spiritual leadership. It is a volume that every Christian leader should possess and read often. Spiritual leaders (influencers), he points out, are not able by themselves to develop or generate superior spiritual power. Rather, they are people through whom the Spirit of God works to perform spiritual results.

In natural leadership, personality plays a primary role. In the spiritual leader, the Holy Spirit takes the natural and God-given qualities of personality and infuses them with spiritual qualities. The modification that occurs produces a release of Spirit-enhanced influence for the glory of God and the good of the church.

While many aspects of natural leadership are similar to spiritual leadership, there are some that are diametrically opposed. Some examples of what Sanders offers as illustration are as follows:[7]

Natural	*Spiritual*
• Self-confident	• Confident in God
• Knows men	• Also knows God
• Makes own decisions	• Seeks to find God's will
• Ambitious	• Self-effacing
• Originates own methods	• Finds and follows God's methods
• Enjoys commanding others	• Delights in obeying God
• Motivated by personal considerations	• Motivated by love for God and man
• Independent	• God-dependent

While it can be argued that that leadership in the church is different in some respects from leadership in general, it is interesting to note that when the Apostle Paul established the qualifications for leaders in the church, he did not center on either spiritual gifts or personal abilities and skills. Rather, Paul chose character qualities.

As another biblical example, when Nehemiah sought a man to

---

7 J. Oswald Sanders, *Spiritual Leadership* (Chicago: Moody Press, 1967, sixth printing) p. 21.

serve as a chief administrator and manager in Jerusalem he chose men who were faithful and devoted to God (Nehemiah 7:2). Character was again the high point on the list. God indicates repeatedly that He wants prepared people and the biblical record shows that God uses prepared people. But above all, Christian leaders in any context must be faithful and devoted to God. Non-profit, religious work is not more spiritual than for-profit work. The heart and the behavior of the leader are what make the difference.

Biblical Qualifications

In looking at what the Bible says about spiritual qualities for leadership, the list can become a little overwhelming. As we try to put the picture together, the number of pieces to the puzzle and the relationships of one to another become more significant. When all the pieces are in place and we step back, the unmistakable image we see before us is a Spirit-controlled leader. That is the divinely intended outcome. Jesus, as the God-man, perfectly filled the role. Paul, Peter, Barnabas and Timothy, to name a few, were in large measure Spirit-controlled leaders. It is interesting to note that nowhere in Scripture does God give us a complete single list and say, "Christian, this is your measuring rod. Fulfill all this and you will be the kind of leader I desire."

God, in His great love and desire for us, has given us a series of statements in Paul's letters to Timothy and Titus and in Peter's first letter. It is interesting to note that the Scriptures never mention physical traits or a brilliant intellect as qualifications for spiritual leadership. From man's perspective, these are paramount. From God's perspective, voluntary obedience, faithfulness and living a holy life in response to the Holy Spirit are paramount in all walks of life.

The biblical qualifications of leadership that are stated or strongly implied can be grouped under the headings of attitude, moral, mental and social life, motives and experience. The list of qualifications below is not meant to be all inclusive, but suggestive of what God is looking for in Spirit-controlled leadership.

Attitude

1. Gentle – one whose life is characterized not by striking out at others and seeking to get even, but is selfless, reasonable and considerate of others.
2. Humble – one who is willing to take on the garment of a servant or slave for the welfare of others.
3. Exemplary – one who is not dictatorial or domineering, but is leading the way as a shepherd and doing whatever is necessary to help people succeed.

Moral Life

1. Purity – one whose life is unscathed, blameless, morally unchallengeable.
2. Temperate – one who consistently exhibits self control and is not addicted to excesses like a drunkard.

Mental Life

1. Prudent – one who practices self-restraint, who has inner control and is sound of mind.
2. Respectable – one who has a good reputation in the community, who has an outer life marked by healthy balance.
3. Able to teach – one who can help those who are at odds with themselves and others to find solutions and answers to the right questions.

Social Life

1. Above reproach – one who has demonstrated consistency in character and interpersonal relationships so people would never think of bringing reproach upon him or her.
2. Good reputation – one who has demonstrated genuine Christian character in all areas of life, especially outside church circles.

Motive

1. Loves to serve – one who is not covetous, nor a lover of money and gain, but is desirous of serving God and people regardless of remuneration.
2. Hospitable – one who helps put others at ease and sees to their comfort, especially strangers; someone that is more than an entertainer, but is a graceful friend.

Experience

1. Mature – one who is not a "newly planted" convert, but one who has experienced some of the storms of testing and stands straight and stronger because of them.
2. Dignity – one who has proven able to live and lead others in a dignified, God-honoring manner.

While this list of qualities and qualifications still seems above us and unattainable in full measure (without the grace and enablement of God, it is), this is not like a mountain peak to be scaled once and then simply remembered into old age. It is a yardstick against which we must continuously measure our inner and outer life and daily be conformed to God's desire and design for us.

Pause and Reflect

Which of the list of biblical leadership qualifications do you have well under control? At which ones do you excel? Which ones do you need to work on as a leader?

We all have strengths and weaknesses in leadership skills, but when it comes to matters of character and spiritual qualities we must strive through God's grace to qualify in every one of them. If there are moral, spiritual, or character issues in your life that need attention, make their improvement a high priority. It will shape everything else that you do.

God wants you to be a success in the same way that He told Joshua so many years ago. Remember, it requires obedience to His word and faithfulness in your daily walk.

Role Models for Leaders

Several models are given in the New Testament that can serve as guides for us as we seek to be Christian leaders, practice Christian leadership and facilitate the development of other Christian leaders. They are the models of the Shepherd, the Servant and the Shipmaster. The Lord Jesus Christ used all three models in His teaching and while they clearly find their context in an agrarian society, they remain instructive for today.

The Shepherd Leader

The most persistent picture presented in Scripture is that of the shepherd and his flock. Of course, in biblical times farming and shepherding were primary ways of life. It is not surprising therefore, that God chose to portray leadership in this way.

In Scripture, forty out of the sixty-six books refer to shepherds and sheep. Some of our favorite Psalms – 22, 23 and 24 – refer to the Good, the Great and the Chief Shepherd. In fact, John 10 gives us great insight into God's perspective on spiritual shepherding as Jesus uses the picture of shepherds and sheep to describe His relationship with people. In this passage Christ calls Himself the Good Shepherd; He is distinguished from all false and counterfeit shepherds (John 10:8); and Peter calls Christ the Chief Shepherd (1 Peter 5:4). The image of Jesus Christ as the shepherd presents us with a potentially productive picture for understanding God's perspective on leadership. Biblical leadership is, therefore, described as shepherding the flock of God.

Shepherd Roles

To understand this better it is helpful to consider a series of biblical statements to get a glimpse of the varied roles shepherds had in biblical times. Fifteen aspects of shepherding have been selected to help us understand some of the privileges and responsibilities and how they apply to leadership. Six of the guidelines come from John

10, six come from Psalm 23 and the remaining three come from Psalm 32 and John 17.

1. *Protection* (John 10:9) The shepherd-leader has a deep interest in the welfare of his people. He has not just hired on because it is a job. He puts himself on the line as the guardian of the flock. Jesus perfectly described His role by choosing the picture of shepherding in ancient Palestine. The shepherds would build a rock fence enclosure with only one small door opening and the sheep would be led into the protection of this enclosure at night. Then, the shepherd himself would lie down in the small door opening and become the door, the protection for the sheep. Leading often involves putting ourselves on the line to guard our team from error and external attacks.

2. *Commitment* (John 10:11) The twin aspect to protection is commitment. Again using the shepherd-leader model, Jesus stated that as the Good Shepherd He was living His life for the sheep, giving it to them so that they grow and prosper. Commitment involves being selfless; thinking and acting in the interests of others more than in your own interests. Jesus lived and ministered persistently, but not in a feverish and uncontrolled manner. His eyes were on the purpose for His coming to earth and He let nothing detract Him from His objective. Likewise, we must clarify our goals and sharpen our commitment.

3. *Personal* (John 10:14a) A pleasant and encouraging experience is to meet someone you have not seen for years and have them remember your name. Jesus said He knew His own. Know your team, their strengths, their weaknesses, but especially their names! If you want to be an effective leader, do not become aloof, detached, or impersonal with your people.

4. *Honesty* (John 10:14b) Not only does the shepherd know the sheep, but he has been open, honest and self-revealing so that they know him. Relationships are built so firmly through personal interaction over a period of time that there is an

exciting reality in the mutual exchange. No guessing as to what the other person might think or do. Openness, honesty and understanding dominate the relationship.

5. *Gives* (John 10:15) Leadership involves building friendships. True friendship is being willing to give of yourself to the utmost (John 15:13). The concept illustrated here is self sacrifice. Jesus had said earlier that He was willing to live for the flock (John 10:11). Now He says He is willing to die for the flock. In many nations around the world today, Christian leaders are actually being called upon to make the ultimate sacrifice.

6. *Communicates* (John 10:16, 27) God has entrusted us with the privilege of communicating His truth. The Bible says that we are His ambassadors or representatives. What we say is a reflection upon Him. At the core of leadership is the ability to communicate well, with careful attention given to accuracy of content, expertise in delivery and purity of attitude.

7. *Concern* (Psalm 23:2a) The shepherd-leader knows the flock must have a balanced life experience. There is a time for work and a time for rest. A wise leader provides times of rest and refreshment for his or her followers, not just times of work. Concern for a healthy balanced life should always prevail in our leadership perspective.

8. *Sensitivity* (Psalm 23:2b) One of the shepherd's duties was to carefully search out places with safe water for the sheep. The shepherd could not take them to swift-running streams since they were easily frightened and if they fell in they would quickly drown. The shepherd would either search out a quiet water area or arrange some stones to form a dam so the needs of the sheep could be met. Sensitivity to people and their needs is a beautiful mark of a biblical leader. It is a sign of wisdom, strength and compassion.

9. *Holiness* (Psalm 23:3) Holiness is to characterize every believer's life, but much more the life of a leader (Leviticus

20:7; Ephesians 1:4; James 3:1). The objective is to lead followers in the paths of right thinking and right acting. Helping others fulfill their God-intended purpose in life means, above all, to help them grow in grace and in the knowledge of Christ Jesus. It means helping them develop the fruit of the Spirit in their lives under the direction and guidance of the Holy Spirit.

10. *Presence* (Psalm 23:4) Of all the great and wonderful promises in Scripture, the one that probably comforts the soul more than any other is the promise of the presence of God (Joshua 1:5; Hebrews 13:5, 6). To know that He is with you at all times brings peace. A great truth for Christian leaders is that we cannot be effective as influencers of others without spending some quality time with our people. One hour once a week will not do it. We must have sufficient quantity time if we are going to have productive quality time. Jesus spent time with His disciples eating, walking, climbing, fishing, visiting, boating, and worshipping. We have to design ways to meet our employees and colleagues in informal settings.

11. *Preparation* (Psalm 23:5) The feeding process of the sheep was not haphazard. Shepherds of old would carefully go over the pasture they intended to use for grazing the sheep, removing harmful plants and constructing barriers to prevent the sheep from wandering into dangerous areas. The shepherd-leader of the human flock must do no less. In the Bible our model is God Himself (Isaiah 40:10, 11). Careful study and mastery of truth is necessary. Knowing the danger areas and providing proper guidelines for our team is essential.

12. *Care* (Psalm 23:6) The sheep of the pasture would occasionally be bruised or cut as they went about their daily chore of feeding and growing. The shepherd would study each one at the end of the day to discover where the hurts were and then apply some healing ointment. The biblical leader of today must be alert to the emotional and spiritual bruises that "the flock"

receives as they go about their daily tasks. A kind word, an encouraging comment, an urging to fight the good fight of faith is needed by all of us. While God will ultimately reward all spiritual deeds, we, as leaders, are to be like shepherds to our people.

13. *Guides* (Psalm 32:8) The shepherd's voice and the shepherd's watch-care are the essential ingredients for safe shepherding. The shepherd does not drive the sheep as a cowboy drives cattle. The shepherd goes before the sheep and guides them by his presence and the path he takes. He is not an autocratic, driving leader. He knows where he is going and leads the way, but the sheep do the walking. He guides the flock to the grass, but the sheep do the grazing. He is not a do-it-yourselfer! He is one who speaks with authority and facilitates the process.

14. *Prays* (John 17) While no specific Scriptural passage indicates that shepherds pray for the animals of their flock, Jesus certainly shows us that He prayed for His human flock as He fulfilled the role of the Good Shepherd. The leader who is not spending time in prayer for the people God has entrusted to his care has totally missed the point of Christian leadership. Prayer sensitizes the leader to both God and man. Prayer is commanded by Jesus and is a source of strength daily.

15. *Loves* (John 17:20-26) The one characteristic that is foundational to all the rest is the fact that the shepherd loves the sheep. The protection, care, commitment and other qualities are tied into the shepherd's unfading love. Love becomes like oil on the gears of a machine. It helps them to mesh without friction and produce the way they were designed to do. Love is not something to be discovered and then left to develop in isolation. To properly mature, love needs careful nurturing. A wise leader is mindful of his commitment to actively love and "courts" his people regularly.

The Servant Leader

Explicit instructions are given by the Lord Jesus with regard to the second model of leadership found in the New Testament. The disciples spent a great deal of time with Jesus. Over three years they heard Him teach, watched him minister to the needy and experienced His leadership. Yet they, like us, had been influenced heavily by the world system around them and assumed that doing God's work was the same as doing the world's work – just with different content. They saw the motives and structures around them and presumed it should be the same way in God's work. Ambition raised its ugly head among them.

Jesus moved quickly to correct their false impressions (Luke 22:24-30). The strife among them had to do with both their immediate and future rank. Jesus said they were to be different from the world system around them. In the world system, leaders (*kurieuo*) exercised authoritarian control over other people. Having people snap to attention in their presence, being rugged and "running a tight ship" were not exactly what Jesus had in mind for the disciples.

Rather, Jesus declared that their leadership role was to be more like a servant. The best definition I know for this word is "one whose life is governed by the bidding of another." They were not to be flashy, pompous, demanding or slick operators. Rather, they were to be as Paul later described in 1 Thessalonians (2:7), gentle as a nursing mother (*herioi*) who softens and warms (*thaloe*) those in her presence. Quite a contrast from what the disciples had been thinking and planning!

Leading is shepherding, but it is also serving. Much is being written these days on servant-leadership. There are a series of implications when we begin to think of leadership in terms of servanthood. A servant is one whose life is lived at the bidding of another, but this does not imply weakness or incompetence. In fact, just the opposite is true. A profitable servant is a skilled, competent, trustworthy and a conscientious worker. What sets apart this servant is his or her attitude. His desire is to see others be successful. Her manner is to facilitate the development of their lives and work. His goal is to be as unobtrusive as possible.

Servant Roles

1. *Skilled* There are a variety of tasks for servants. At times a servant must perform diverse functions and be able to multitask well. At other times the servant is a specialist, called upon to fill one specific role: a cook, a gardener or a chauffeur. The same is true in ministry. A biblical servant must be equipped for spiritually good and maturing work.

2. *Competent* A biblical leader is qualified, first by personal faith in Jesus Christ, and second, by a felt call to the work of service. We often ask ourselves, who is sufficient for such a calling? The answer comes back – we are made sufficient through a close personal walk with the Lord. There is an ongoing maturing process that produces competency as it develops.

3. *Trustworthy* To be trusted is a greater compliment than to be loved. The biblical leader must be a person of integrity, veracity and confidence. Another biblical term that parallels this is faithfulness. We should be found faithful in living and working. People need leaders who will be true to their word and work.

4. *Conscientious* Having an inner sensitivity to doing what is right demands a clear and God-tuned conscience. A biblical leader will have high principles and seek to not only personally abide by these principles, but to instill them in the lives of others. A commitment to work and diligence in performing the work, marks the servants of the Lord.

Servant Directions (Luke 22:24-27)

Jesus Christ sets forth very clear directions in Luke 22 as to a biblical leader's motivating force. The disciples argued among themselves in their ongoing rivalry. They apparently had a pattern of strife and verbal attacks and were seeking special favors and political positions. We have all seen this type of maneuvering!

Our Lord first describes the persistent behavior of the rulers of secular society and in so doing, implies that the disciples' behavior is the same. The leadership approach of the secularist is summed up in the word *kurieuo* which in simple terms means to exercise authoritarian control over others.

Christ then declares that the biblical leader's behavior is not to be that of an overlord, but rather that of a servant. He further accentuates His point by clearly stating that His own role was one of serving. Caring for the welfare of the group, seeing to it that the needs of the group are being met, facilitating by careful planning and gentle guidance, the biblical leader-servant does God's work God's way.

A servant-leader is a worker, not simply a teller. This type of leader teaches by example, by modeling, by demonstrating the acts of God in attitude and action. The leader who seeks to serve, leads without manipulation of others nor magnification of self.

To have a powerful impact on someone else normally requires that individual to have frequent, long-term contact that takes place in a variety of situations and is generally marked by a consistent and carefully designed set of values and beliefs. These are demonstrated in the leader's actions and patterns of behavior. Just as learning does not take place in a vacuum but in the practical experiences of everyday living and working, so here the leader teaches by example through consistent behavior and the presentation of principled beliefs. The servant leader is consistent in seeking the best for and from his fellow workers. A pattern of dependable and consistent actions reinforces the truths he has presented. This teaching by example helps reinforce the truths and impact those on the team. The servant leader model is a favorite example for scores of leadership and management teachers and authors.

The Shipmaster – The Manager-Leader

The third model given in Scripture is brief in its appearance, but powerful in its meaning. It is the term chosen by Paul to describe the gift of administration in the early church. The term used is *kubernetes* which literally means, "to steer a ship." The term refers to the one who, either is the owner of the ship or on behalf of the ship's owner, guides the ship, makes the critical decisions necessary for the welfare of the ship, crew, passengers and cargo and thus is the equivalent of our modern-day captain.

Leaders who seek to be consistent Christian leaders are ones who realize that they are created by God, prepared by God, chosen by God and called by God to the work of leadership. They are responsible for those entrusted to their care which means that they make decisions prayerfully but always based on their knowledge and experience. This picture of a decision maker who takes seriously their responsibility for knowing every key aspect of the journey, adds an important dimension to our understanding of the biblical leader. In addition to the models of the shepherd and servant, this is an insightful picture of the manager-leader.

In a related way, there are the concepts of planning, organizing, leading and directing embraced in the ruler role of Romans 12:8 and the faithfulness criteria set forth for the house-manager in 1 Corinthians 4:2. The "shipmaster" as a leader-manager model should not be seen in isolation from the other models. However, when combined with the equalities of the shepherd and servant models, it adds an important dimension to our understanding of leadership.

What follows is a series of roles and functions that are most obvious in the "shipmaster," manager-leader aspect of leadership. What is best is an understanding that today's godly leader seeks to blend the three different models of leadership presented in the Bible into one consistent and complete picture. Realizing that different circumstances call for different responses, the godly leader seeks to maintain a godly perspective in whatever situation arises. Responding as a servant may be appropriate in one situation while responding as a manager or shipmaster may be better in another setting. Maintaining the shepherd's heart in all settings is also appropriate.

Manager Roles

Consider the manager-leaders roles:

1. *Decision-maker* A critical aspect of the biblical manager-leader role is the ability to make decisions when necessary. Even in the secular world, the manager who can make decisions is rated an effective manager and those who procrastinate in this area receive a very low rating.

   Solomon persistently refers to the necessity of wise leadership, meaning managers who can make decisions based on the appropriate gathering of information (Proverbs 1:5; 11:14; 24:6). The biblical manager also clearly recognizes that every decision he or she makes affects the future behavior and welfare of others. They are, therefore, properly sensitive as well as properly decisive.

   One of the dangers in this aspect of leadership is the abuse of power exercised by some leaders who make decisions only on the basis of materialistic gain or personal exaltation. These are not the motivations of the Biblical leader. The glory of God and the good of the people are our twin guidelines. Material profit growth and gain is not wrong in itself. It is wrong, however, if sought in a biblically unprincipled manner. Even the numerical growth of a church can be pursued in ways that are not good for believers or for the testimony of God's name.

2. *Detailer* Paul's instruction in Romans 12:8 specifically declares that he who manages must give care to the details of his assignment. Clearly, a wise manager sees the whole picture but also knows the details involved. A godly leader guides with a twofold perspective. They constantly have in mind both the larger picture of the cause of Christ and greater glory of God, as well as the minute details of what has to happen to cause that larger picture to become a reality. They must neglect neither.

3. *Faithful* In each of the three primary models or pictures of leadership, the aspect of faithfulness is clear. For the manager,

however, it is specifically stated as a criterion of success from God's perspective. In 1 Corinthians chapter four, Paul points out that Christian leaders are evaluated ultimately by God and that the criterion is faithfulness.

We are prone to measure accomplishment by numbers and material acquisition and size. This is a very finite viewpoint. God's perspective is different and we must see success as God sees it. Doing what we are supposed to do in our living and our working is our responsibility. The results are in God's hands.

The Biblical Leader

I believe that the biblical leader needs to be a balanced blend of a shepherd's heart, a servant's attitude and a shipmaster's mind. Without balance, a person can become eccentric, or focus on one aspect of leadership to the exclusion of the other parts of the leader's role. This type of leader will produce an off-balanced group of people who look to him or her as a model and only see one part of the biblical mandate. Being too sharply focused, the leader may have a prime concern for making a profit, numerical growth, caring for one another, or even acquisition of Biblical knowledge. Each one of these are valid goals but as isolated concerns they are incomplete. They need to be seen in context. A leader must always be concerned with the big picture.

A balanced biblical leader will model the loving, serving, faithfully empowering type of leader who produces a healthy, growing group of followers that demonstrate in their life and their work a commitment to God. They are models of integrity, productivity and seek to both please God and serve others, and this world needs more of them.

Pause and Reflect

While the biblical model is a blend of three different types or roles from ancient days, today's leader has the benefit of learning from all of them and discovering the joy of leadership in practice.

Which of the three models do you think best represents your primary approach to leadership? What are your strengths and which leadership traits do you still need to work on? Have you surrounded yourself with leaders who have strengths in the areas of your weaknesses? How have you profited from this approach? How do you practically blend each model together in your daily work?

Finally, who has influenced you the most as a leader and helped shape your life? Sit down and write them a note of appreciation and encouragement. God places people all around us to help us grow and mature. Give thanks today to the Lord and those He has placed in your path.

CHAPTER 2

ORGANIZATIONAL
LEADERSHIP

LEADERS face a myriad of tasks in the workplace every day. Few are as critical to the success of the organization as ensuring that the organization is committed to clear mission and vision statements which are understood and embraced throughout the enterprise. These two vital management documents are informed and guided by a set of core values which help give direction to the mission and vision statements.

The strategic plan is the practical implementation of these foundational organizational commitments. This chapter sets forth basic concepts to help the leader develop, review, or revise existing management documents to constantly improve the company's performance.

Establishing a Vision

When an enterprise wants to be successful, make a significant contribution to their unique industry and become a profitable endeavor, they eventually realize the importance of identifying, confirming and promoting their vision, mission and core values along with the development of a strategic plan to carry out the process. These are not simply management exercises, but rather necessary leadership steps that will help the organization stay on course, make a difference in their field and increase profits or improve services.

It may seem obvious to some that a college exists for education, a church for worship, or an assembly plant to manufacture cars; but a wise leader knows that each of these organizations are specific social groupings, in a certain period of time, with defined historical backgrounds and inherited cultural compositions, that make each of them special and unique, even if they have similar organizations in competition. Defining that uniqueness and positioning the organization to have a long and productive future means thinking and planning ahead with discernment and purpose.

While developing a mission statement is typically the first step, establishing the vision is critical in determining the long range development of the organization. For that reason we will look at the vision statement first, followed by mission statement, core values and strategic planning.

The mission statement clarifies what the organization is designed to be and do. It answers the question, "Why do we exist and what do we do?" The answer to this question may have been very obvious to the founders but as the years go by this clarity can become fuzzy and actually get lost over time. An organization's core values dictate why it does what it does as they determine the direction of the vision. Generally, the vision statement will be the expansion and development view of the future of the company. Finally, the strategic planning process deals with how a group will implement its mission and its vision. Without a clear, practical strategy, organizations do not accomplish their vision or their mission with surety or efficiency.

The visioning process should take place at multiple levels within an organization. Personal vision is an individual leader's unique contribution and commitment to the company and comes as a result of discovering one's purpose for living and working. This usually consists of a combination of spiritual gifts, natural talents, passion, temperament, leadership style and other things that make up the individual leader. The identification of a personal vision not only helps the leader in general but is a powerful force in helping others understand the leader more accurately and determine their own commitment to and place within the business.

Organizational vision relates to the business of a particular organization. Once a leader has determined his or her personal vision, he can better identify and align his vision with the organizational vision. When personal vision and organizational vision are aligned, the resulting synergy produces a variety of advantages. It lessens the likelihood of leadership burnout and strengthens the productivity of both leader and company. Personal and institutional visions are equally essential.

Definition and Characteristics of Vision

Organizational vision is a clear and challenging picture of the future of the company. It is a snapshot of the future, so to speak. The vision must be explicit and clear. Team members have to understand it well enough to be able to explain it to others and corporate leaders will take every opportunity to present the vision as often as possible so others can share in the progress. The more the vision can be described in practical and physical terms, the easier it is to communicate.

Next, the vision needs to be challenging and cause the organization to grow and improve. A vision is a desired future; it is a stretching type of experience. Every organization is started by a visionary or entrepreneur who eventually passes from the scene, normally taking their original vision with them. In both profit oriented and non-profit oriented organizations that no longer have access to that first vision, many people hold on to the present experience and do not dream about the future. This can cause stagnation. A vision is valuable because it helps challenge people to think futuristically and then begin to plan for a specific future.

Vision is a "seeing" word. A good vision probes the imagination in such a way that it conjures up visual representations in the mind. It helps people form a mental picture of a possible future. Vision is an act of seeing; it is an imaginative perception combining insight and foresight. As a picture, it is pointing to the future. It is presented in words that describe what tomorrow will look like with its possibilities and potentialities. There are both short term vision statements and long term vision statements. Most vision statements are constantly in a state of becoming and therefore remain futuristic. They are intended to draw people forward to consider new horizons.

While visioning is a future-oriented process, a good vision must rest on a foundation of facts and reality. As such, it must be within the scope and resources of the group – both present and future – in order to be accomplished. On the one hand, when there is little or no vision, organizations can plateau and die because their leadership has no view of future possibilities. On the other hand, a vision can be too big. Some people will not give the vision a fair hearing because it is so immense that it tends to overwhelm them. They can feel intimidated and defeated just listening to it. On the other hand, if the vision is not realistic, they will feel disillusioned and discouraged if it does not come to pass. Organizational instability can often be traced to a lack of a clear, realistic and deliverable vision.

How can we determine the right size for an organization's vision? First it is important to note that, generally speaking, most visions are not big enough. However, the answer to this question is affected by the answers to several prior questions. The first is who is doing the visioning. Is the person creating the vision statement able – by virtue of ability and position – to help make the vision a reality?

Next, who are the people that make up the leadership team for the business? Do they share and believe in the vision? Are they working on the type of business or program plans that reinforce the things needed to accomplish the vision?

And finally, is the economic, social and technological time right for the vision to be realized? Great ideas sometimes fail because the leaders have not accurately assessed the potential in the enterprises climate.

To summarize, a vision that motivates and pulls an organization or business forward is a *must be* type of statement. A good vision statement grabs hold and won't let go. Not only does the visionary believe it, but he or she is convinced that it *must be*. If the leader is a Christian, he or she will normally believe that God is involved in it. Believers focus on the truth that if a vision is valid, God must be the motivating force behind it. For a Christian leader, the vision needs to glorify God and further His kingdom in some apparent way. Thus, organizational vision is a clear, challenging picture of the future that both the leader and the team believe *must be*.

By gathering and reviewing a number of different vision statements, you will begin to understand the purpose and power that a clear, realistic and practical vision can provide for a company. In today's fast paced world, tomorrow becomes today's business and the future is now.

Pause and Reflect

Gather a few vision statements from similar organizations comparable to yours. If your organization has a vision statement, compare theirs to yours. What is similar? What is distinctive about yours?

If you do not have a vision statement for your group, start working on one now. Share your ideas with a few key leaders in you circles and begin to share your ideas with other employees to get buy-in and additional ideas. Once you have settled on a statement that you are comfortable with, post it in several prominent places around the building. Use it in various publications, newsletters, etc. and after a period of time (six months to a year) review it, revise it and confirm it as your working document.

The Benefits of Visioning

Since time and money will be invested in the process of developing a vision statement and vision plan, it is important to identify the potential benefits for your business or organization. If there is no return on investment, the stakeholders will likely reject such a process. Remember that a well crafted vision statement will help the leadership clarify the enterprises' direction. A vision is a picture of the future, but it is created out of the core values of the organization and is directional in its emphasis. Leaders must know where they are going and the people must have a clear understanding of the company's direction if they are to work together as a team. People need clarity to be able to focus. Just as a photographer must see clearly through the camera lens in order to get a good picture, leaders must know what they are setting out to accomplish. That is what a good vision statement will provide.

Another benefit from a good vision statement is that it can help unify the organization's work force. This often involves the recruitment and retention of personnel and the best use of employees' skills and gifts in pursuit of the company vision. If regularly communicated, the vision statement serves as a constant reminder to people of the direction they have agreed to pursue together as a team. This is important because life is full of changes. The workforce often undergoes many changes in its makeup and even the people who remain are changing constantly. When the vision is clear, the people who make up the organization at any given time need to be able to understand and commit to its future direction in light of their own abilities and personal directions in life. As a leader you have probably already discovered that a clear anticipation of what is the business' future will help focus the team.

What are we all about? One of the problems in some groups is that they do not know what they are supposed to be doing. Some people have changed jobs within the organization and may question their present function. Others may ask, "What are we supposed to be doing?" Clear vision and mission statements should help answer those questions. People will also ask things like, "What is the place going to look like ten years from now?" A clear vision statement communicates all of this and provides people with a visual image of what the future may look like.

Further, a vision can enhance the image and work of the leadership. Developing a vision and then living it vigorously and authentically are essential elements of effective leadership. A Christian leader is to be a godly servant who has character, who knows and sees where he or she is going (mission and vision) and has followers (to influence).

A clear presentation of the organization's vision will help focus both planning and passion in any business, whether it is for-profit or non-profit. One problem that leaders face regularly is mediocrity. Not enough attention is given to details that make a difference. Meetings are sometimes poorly planned and poorly executed; agendas are not carefully considered or designed. Job assignments may be inefficiently created and so conflicts can arise because people do not know what they are supposed to do and what things they are to avoid. Numerous studies have indicated that vision and passion work hand in hand. While vision is a seeing word that involves what leaders envision in their near and far futures, passion is a feeling word that involves their emotions and what they feel in their hearts. Vision (seeing) and passion (feeling) must be united to produce leaders who have informed commitment to achievable goals.

A vision statement, because it is future oriented, encourages a degree of risk taking. Some may question whether or not this is a benefit! All leaders know that taking risks is a necessary part of their job but equally important is making sure that the risks are worth taking. Since a vision is a picture of a preferred future it is subject to all sorts of changes and uncertainties. Any type of vision will be a risk venture. Every believer listed in Hebrews 11, faith's "hall of fame," was apparently willing to take a vision-engendered risk.

To see a more practical side of the issue, note that a vision offers a degree of stability and strength. One of the great problems some groups experience is the onset of discouragement and disappointment. This occurs due to the repetitive nature of the work and the setbacks that can take place along the way. What is able to keep individuals going under difficult circumstances is a compelling vision of the future. It encourages people to look beyond the mundane as it holds out a picture that distracts us from present problems and loudly announces "This is what could be!"

A vision also has the capacity to create energy. Nothing much happens without inspiring and compelling vision. One of my favorite biblical characters is Nehemiah. The record of his leadership in the book that bears his name is a perfect example of how one man's vision and leadership can overturn the lethargy that sets in when people are not motivated by a clear picture of what could be. Nehemiah was moved by the Lord to request a leave from his important position in Persia and travel to Jerusalem. His vision was to lead the people in rebuilding the wall of Jerusalem and to revive city life and worship; and he did exactly that. Nehemiah provided them with a view of what could be done at a time when they were discouraged and felt defeated. Visions are exciting and energizing. They strengthen and invigorate people. They strike a spark of excitement that lifts both people and businesses out of the mundane and propels them forward.

Finally, a well developed and agreed upon vision can provide significant purpose for the organization and the people who work in it. It can give a sense of being part of something great and something bigger than ourselves. A good vision is also beneficial for the financial health of the organization. Clients are more likely to support the enterprise if they believe that there is a future to the business and that it will maintain the principles and practices that drew them to the business in the first place. With a careless and impersonal climate developing in the marketplace in recent years, people are looking for organizations they can trust and support. Wise leaders will put their best foot forward and promote their strengths and deliver on their plans and projections. That means there must be a clear statement of whom they are and where they are going as a business. It proclaims that the best is yet to come.

Pause and Reflect

Review your use of your vision statement with top leaders in the organization. Discuss it with different groups of employees and solicit their input as to its relevance and practicality. Decide on a strategy for using it more effectively and develop a plan for action. Use the statement in various public presentations and documents.

Visionary Leadership

Organizations that want to not only survive but prosper need visionary leadership. One of the marks of a visionary leader is the fact that, while they often articulate their personal mission statement, they tend to focus much more on the vision statement of the organization. While they deal with the day-to-day operational issues, their minds are continually processing the potentials that lie ahead. Bureaucratic and politically oriented leaders need to surround themselves with some visionary people and heed their counsel if they want to be successful. Knowing the difference between mission (what we are all about) and vision statements (what we are designing to be in the future) is important.

There are a number of differences between a vision statement and a mission statement. First, a mission statement is more of a declaration of what the business is all about. It generally begins with the words, "The XYZ business exists for the purpose of...." A vision statement is a description or a word picture or snapshot of a specific time in the future that describes the intended future of the business. It usually will have words like, "The XYZ business will be...." The mission statement points to the present while the vision statement points to a preferred future.

The uses for the two statements also differ. The mission statement is a control device, primarily used to keep the organization on target and avoid sidetracking endeavors that can reduce the effectiveness and resources of the company. The mission statement is used in the planning process. The vision statement, on the other hand, is a way of communicating to employees, clients and the industry at large the future orientation of the business. It is a communication device and useful in the strategic planning process.

Another difference between mission and vision statements is their length. Mission statements are short and informative; one to three sentences that can be posted, memorized and promoted regularly throughout the business to keep everyone focused on their main objectives. Vision statements are generally longer, more descriptive and used primarily to inspire, motivate and help stakeholders visualize their intended future. One stresses doing while the other stresses seeing. Someone described the difference between them as the difference between the head and the heart; the mind and the emotions. In communicating the two, the mission statement is more taught, while the vision statement is more caught. Both are important and need executive attention and promotion.

Every effective leader is forward looking and generally able to see into the future far enough to anticipate what challenges and opportunities the enterprise will likely face as time goes by. In fact, that is the very meaning of being visionary. While a leader is obviously involved in the present operation, they must be looking to the horizon to anticipate what will be the next development in their field. They must be looking for what new technology might bring so they will be ready to excel in both the immediate and long range futures.

Once the leader has a mental picture of what lies ahead, they must be able to put into visual form through words, charts, or pictures what that preferred future will look like. It needs to be presented in a most positive manner, showing the values, benefits and uniqueness of the business and how those things can be applied to the future development and expansion of the company's value and effectiveness. A visionary leader excites, motivates and enables the team to dream and commit to a potential that is real, though not yet realized.

In the Bible there is a wonderful example of a vision statement. God provided Moses with a vision of the future and Moses communicated it to his people by saying, "For the LORD your God is bringing you into a good land – a land with streams and pools of water, with springs flowing in the valleys and hills; a land with wheat and barley, vines and fig trees, pomegranates, olive oil and honey; a land where bread will not be scarce and you will lack nothing; a land where the rocks are iron and you can dig copper out of the hills" (Deuteronomy 8:7-10). The Israelites were able to see, with the mind's eye, the goal toward which they were heading and they began to move forward.

This text also demonstrates the importance of maintaining the vision. The Israelites were not very far down the path when they decided to look backward and not forward. Moses encouraged them to look to the "land that flows with milk and honey," as he attempted to keep the vision of the people focused on the end result and not the present pressures. Even today, visionary leaders realize that to keep the dream alive there must be a plan that persistently pursues the future with visual support and clear goals.

This is a good time to think about how this material influences us in the daily routines of executive life and business situations. Here are a few questions to be considered by leaders at all levels in every enterprise:

1. Do the values, abilities and goals of your life align with those of your organization?
2. What skills and abilities do you have that can help foster organization growth and development over the next five to ten years?
3. What are your limitations or deficiencies in skills, abilities, or personal traits that might hold back the company from forward progress?
4. What is your organization's uniqueness and strongest contribution to your industry and community?
5. What does your business or organization need to do to overcome present operating weaknesses in order to become more effective and more profitable?

6. What is the one thing that, if it could be changed, would produce the greatest forward progress for your company?
7. Are there any processes or procedures that are hindering the quality performance of your best employees?
8. Is there a plan and program in place to improve worker performance and total organization productivity?

These are reflective questions, designed to help executives review and improve a group's productivity, employee satisfaction and overall reputation and value to the various stakeholders. Each one should be answered carefully and fully.

Pause and Reflect

Use these additional questions to guide your analysis of your performance and to help you gauge the effectiveness of the other team members.

1. *What is the level of urgency in your group to incrementally improve products and services? (If you and other leaders of your organization are fairly con-tent with the current level of effectiveness, the process of establishing a vision will be of little value.)*

2. *Who are the impact players on your leadership team? How can you enhance their contribution?*

3. *What core values are most important to you and the leadership team?*

4. *When you talk to employees and the leadership, what topics excite you the most?*

5. *What would you identify as truly unique in your organization?*

6. *What products, services, or policies set you apart from others in your industry?*

7. *If you were forced to choose only one product or service, which one would you keep?*

8. *State in one sentence your vision for your organization.*

9. *Who in your company have you chosen to be involved in defining or honing your organizational vision? Why were they chosen?*

10. *Who makes up your inner circle in your operation?*

11. *How and when will you move forward in implementing your revised vision statement?*

Organizational Mission

When I was called to the presidency of Lancaster Bible College one of my early and primary concerns was to work through with the faculty, the mission statement of the college. Numerous faculty and committee meetings were devoted to defining and refining the mission statement. After more than a year of careful discussion the statement was submitted to the board of the college for ratification. Even at this level it underwent more examination and refinement. It finally became, *"Lancaster Bible College exists for the purpose of educating Christian men and women to live according to a biblical worldview and serve in professional Christian ministry."* It defined us as a professional collegiate level school with a biblically centric purpose. For over 25 years it went unchanged and guided every curriculum modification, hiring practice, lifestyle guideline and the entire campus culture. Mission clarification is critical.

But as I have noted earlier, vision is not the same as mission. They are closely related, but different in purpose and length. While vision is a compelling image of a more desirable future; mission deals with what the organization is now. Vision generates energy and ignites passion; mission exercises energy and organizational passion in order to work. The mission of the company is as clear a statement as can be made of the company's reason for existence. It is to be practical, concrete and regularly reviewed for relevancy. A good mission statement can help keep the business and the work performed by employees on target, for it stresses the purpose in clear and tangible forms. A mission statement helps to make the vision statement real and realizable.

A mission is the reason for the existence of the business or organization. It is the way we understand the purpose for our existence. Mission statements of organizations will be as varied as the industries and personalities of those who run them. The management of all kinds of companies requires both the assessment of what the primary task of the organization is and what it can be in the days ahead.

There are a number of steps in the development of a mission statement for an organization. First, is the clarification of the central reason for the enterprise's existence. This is usually distilled by a group of leaders as they discuss the need for the services and products potentially produced by the firm, its resources, its values and the nature of the business as it was originally created. If the organization is an existing one, it means reviewing the original organizational steps and reaching a preliminary consensus as to the primary task of the business.

Next is the identification of the needs that are not being met by some other related type of business. This is often followed by posing a preliminary mission statement that attempts to complete the sentence, "XYZ exists for the purpose of...." The statement should contain a future element which the phrase "for the purpose of" usually suggests; however, the statement is really a present-oriented concept.

The mission statement is an attempt at describing the nature of the business, the delivery system of the business in the broadest terms possible and the intended end results. It expresses the essential essence of the organization in general terms but specific enough to distinguish it from other groups that are in the same type of business. It should be clear enough to let people know the business focus, reason for existence and intended end results whether they are services or products. Once the statement has been crafted and examined for accuracy and relevance, it should be unveiled in a formal manner and made visible for internal and external use. The mission statement is the type of document that is fairly stable and long-lasting. Yet despite this stability, the mission statement should continue to be reviewed on a regular basis, with one to five years being a normal time frame. The reason for this is to first insure that the company is fulfilling the statement's intentions and second to discover whether or not the mission statement is in need of revision to guarantee accuracy.

The importance of a mission statement is illustrated in the story of an old life saving station.[8] Once upon a time, on a dangerous seacoast where shipwrecks often occurred, there was once a crude little lifesaving station. The building was just a hut and there was only one boat, but the few devoted members kept a constant watch over the sea. Without personal consideration for their own safety, they went out day and night to rescue those in danger on the sea. Many lives were saved by this wonderful little station and it became famous. Other folks in the surrounding area, including some who had been saved, wanted to become associated with the station and give time and money and effort to support its work. New boats were purchased and new crews trained. The little lifesaving station grew.

Some of the members of the lifesaving station were unhappy that the importance of the place was so crude and poorly equipped. They felt that a more attractive and comfortable place should be provided as the first refuge of those saved from the sea. As a result, they replaced the emergency cots with beds and put better furniture in the enlarged building. Now the lifesaving station became a popular gathering place for its members. They continued to improve the station, decorating it beautifully and furnishing it exquisitely. As time went on, it began to resemble a club more than a life saving

---

8 The *Parable of the Lifesaving Station* is a traditional illustration, originally authored by Theodore Wedel, an Episcopal priest in 1953. Since then, it has been repeated, revised and modified by countless authors.

station. Fewer members were now interested in going to sea on life-saving missions, so they hired lifeboat crews to do this work.

The lifesaving motif still prevailed in this club's decorations and there was even a lifeboat placed in the room where club initiations were held. About this time a large ship was wrecked off the coast and the hired crews brought in boatloads of cold, wet, half-drowned people. They were dirty and sick, of different races and cultures. The beautiful new club was in chaos. So the property committee imme-diately had a shower house built outside the club where shipwreck victims could be cleaned up before coming inside.

At the next meeting, there was a division in the club membership. Most of the members wanted to stop the club's lifesaving activities because they were unpleasant and a hindrance to the normal social life of the club. Some members insisted upon lifesaving as their primary purpose and pointed out that they were still called a life-saving station. But they were finally voted down and told that if they wanted to save the lives of all the different kinds of people who were shipwrecked in those waters, they could begin their own lifesaving station down the coast. They did.

As the years went by, the new station experienced the same changes that had occurred in the old. It evolved into a club and yet another lifesaving station was founded. History continued to repeat itself and if you visit that seacoast today, you will find a number of exclusive clubs along that shore. Shipwrecks are still fairly frequent in those waters, but most of the people drown.

The point of the illustration is clear. Without a defining mission an organization can clearly drift into uncertainty and then useless-ness. The application is that most organizations go through a similar scenario. Some businesses lose their focus, some colleges change their direction and some charities lose their purpose. In the 1970s, writing a mission statement became a popular exercise. The experi-ence made a difference for many organizations but for others, the mission statement was largely ignored after it was written. It was an exercise that was valuable at the time but successors failed to see the importance of the process and thus many businesses began to drift and lose their focus because they did not maintain their relevance or seek to renew and reinvigorate the process.

A mission statement defines the business or organization and targets the resources. To be effective, mission statements must be clear, truthful and reflect the contemporary situation. They must answer the three questions: 1) Who are we? 2) What is our business, and 3) How do we get it done? These questions were first suggested by Peter Drucker, who held that because these questions are so rarely asked in a clear and focused form, they are seldom given adequate study and thought. Every business leader should ask these basic questions and lead the organization in a continuous process of self renewal. A wise executive once said that the primary responsibility of leadership is to keep the business and the work performed by the people on target. The mission statement is a target statement. We need to keep our focus clear so the communication of our commitments through the mission statement can be one of our most useful tools.

Pause and Reflect

Review, revise if necessary and then revisit your mission statement with a few key leaders to see if it accurately describes your present reason for existence. Evaluate each word to be sure of clarity, accuracy and meaning.

Review where and how you use the statement in the company to insure that all employees fully understand it. Test your policies and procedures by it to verify that all the official documents are consistent in their message. Be sure to have the board, or the partners, review the mission statement annually to perpetuate the company's purpose and focus.

Basic Organizational Elements

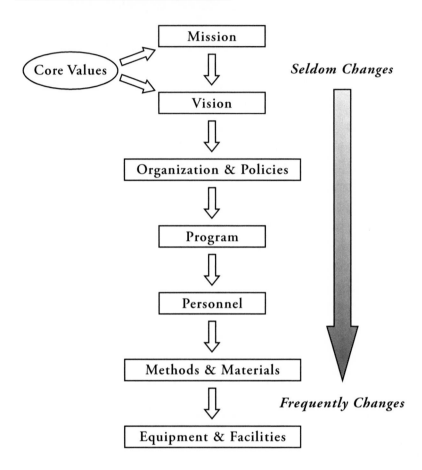

Basic Organizational Chart explanation

This organizational chart puts the mission statement at the very top because it states why the organization exists. Next is the vision statement because it describes where the organization wants to be in the future. Both are significantly influenced by the core values. Next is the organization's structure and policies which are established by the leadership and guide the operation. The next part of the structure is the program or programs that are designed to carry out the organization's mission. Then personnel are needed to implement the programs using the methods and materials selected for the program. Finally, and what should be the most flexible elements in the entire organization, even though they might seem to be fairly permanent, are the equipment and facilities with and within which the organization operates. The top elements are the most permanent and long lasting whereas the bottom elements can change and be adapted as technology advances.

Organizational Core Values

Core values are the constant, passionate beliefs that drive leaders and companies. There are many ways to begin to consider the topic of core values but a couple of key questions are: "What are the non-negotiable beliefs for which you would be willing to die?" and "Which of these would have a significant effect your business operation?" Core values are the building blocks of your philosophy of life, even if you have never actually written such a document. Core values are what you believe about things like life, eternity, people, truth, integrity and commitment. While they are grounded in your religious beliefs, they expand to include your working procedures, goals and relationships. They are not your reason for existence but they influence the direction of your life and work in significant ways.

Everyone has core values, whether or not they have articulated them. For the leader who professes to be a Christian, core values are grounded and find their source in the Bible. Those of other faiths will take core values from their own sacred beliefs and writings. Those who profess not to believe in a Supreme Being will have their core values grounded in personal experience or some rationalistic formula. The reason for stating core values clearly and in writing is to be able to examine them and share them with those whom you lead. The more we understand each other, our beliefs, skills, backgrounds and abilities, the more effectively we can work together and appreciate each other's contribution to the success of the business.

In the Bible God presents values for human life. He also provides us with the values that should under gird Christian leadership. The Bible presents leaders in several models or patterns. For example, leaders are presented as servants in Mark 10:43-44; as shepherds in John 21:17; as trainers in Ephesians 4:12; as mentors in Galatians 6:1; as teachers in 2 Timothy 2:2; as managers in Titus 1:7 and as correctors and encouragers in 2 Timothy 4:2. Christian leaders are told to value truth in John 8:32; care for the needs of others in John 21:16 and worship God in Philippians 3:3. These are only a few of the many expectations for godly leaders, but all are designed to make the Christian leader a person who is compassionate, competent and committed.

Expanding the base of core values, the Scriptures set forth such things as love, integrity, truthfulness, patience, excellence, holiness, unity, prayer and many other personal and spiritual values for leaders to examine and practice. While it is important to know what core values are, it is also instructive to know what they are not. Core values are not vision statements. A vision answers the question "What are we going to do in the future?" whereas a core value answers the question "Why do we do what we do?"

One way of clarifying this distinction is to recognize that every business or organization should be vision-focused and values-driven. A vision focuses on the future and gives direction, but the values are what shape the principles, sharpen the process, provide direction toward the preferred destination and bring things into clear view. Every group will normally have some set of values, even though not clearly identified and articulated, but they may not have a vision. A vision focuses on the future, but values look to the present or the past. Values deal primarily with what has been embraced as truth in the past.

Core values are not a set of principles or a strategic plan. Values provide the foundation upon which principles are based. For example, a common core value for many Christians who have a family business is the importance of having a strong family life with biblically based commitments. A biblical principle that might serve as a general guideline for this could be Proverbs 29:17, "Discipline your son, and he will give you peace; he will bring delight to your soul." Having valid, biblically based values, rules and guidelines for family life becomes an important factor for many leaders. The implementation of the principle is also critical. The vision question asks, "What are we doing?" The strategy question is "How are we going to do it?" But the values question asks, "Why are we going to do it?" Understanding the difference between these three concepts can lead to greater effectiveness.

Characteristics of Core Values

Core values are stable elements in the management scheme. A constant in life is the reality of change. Knowing that, it is vital for leaders to recognize what is appropriate to change and what is not. Being flexible is a good thing in many areas. A good leader is one who knows how to bend and adjust to changing circumstances and different personalities in life and work. However there are some things that are not negotiable in life and work. Some of these include concerns like safety issues, moral commitments and honesty and fairness in treating other people. Having a well thought-through and implemented set of core values can help keep a business from straying from the path of integrity and losing sight of its God-intended purpose.

Core values are emotional and can even be passionate elements in a company culture. Passion is a feeling word. A good core value touches the heart and elicits strong emotions. It moves you and stirs in you an excitement that can motivate you to action. Generally, a value is an intellectual element in that it appeals to the mind. However, a core value is also passionate in that it affects how you feel as much as what you think. People who share your values tend to feel the same way toward them as you do. When they hear you speak about such values in a meeting, they connect with you on a deep level. There is a sense of a kindred spirit that can make your appeal attractive to them. Core values do more than stir emotions and make you passionate, they arouse you to action. It is inspirational and adds value to whatever you say and do.

Finally, for the confessed Christian leader, core values are biblical and central to your entire belief system. Core values can be either sacred or secular. The difference is their source. Sacred values find their origin in God and generally are presented in the Bible. Secular values, for those who separate the secular and the sacred, find their origin in rationality and in the natural realm. In the Middle Ages, there arose a false dichotomy between the things considered sacred and the things considered secular. It arose due to the religious form of separating monastic life from regular societal living. For example, Roman Catholic priests who lived apart in strict separation from the rest of life were called sacred priests, while other Roman Catholic priests who worked outside the church in society were called secular priests.

When God created the world no secular or sacred dichotomy existed as all of God's creation was sacred. However, the so-called secular realm came into existence (as recorded in Genesis 3: 4) when Satan spoke the first lie and seduced Adam and Eve with the statement, "You will not surely die." Secular, therefore, generally refers to anything which is not under submission to Jesus Christ, or any area of thought and life that is not under the control and influence of the Holy Spirit. Things are often considered sacred or secular depending on the motive and controlling influence.

The Devil, the one the Bible calls Satan, is the author of secularism. Presently he controls our secular world and much of what takes place in it, according to Ephesians 2:1-3. He is identified in the Bible as the father of lies in John 8:44 and thus logically, everything that is in the secular realm is tainted with this fatal flaw. It is critical to recognize, therefore, that secular values, no matter how subtle or insignificant or seemingly innocent they appear to be, are false. They are harmful to any Christian who is in business or organization that wants to maintain a Christian testimony.

Sacred values, on the other hand, are biblical values that find their origin in God. Since the Bible tells us that God is true and unchangeable, He will always remain true. It follows then that core values which are part of a Christian leader's position must be grounded in the Scriptures. It would also follow then that a business leader's core values and the core values of a Christian family business will be rooted in their core beliefs. A belief is a conviction or opinion that you hold to be true, based on some evidence or proof. It is also true that it is something that you trust, or in which you have placed your faith. A belief is not a fact, by definition. However, a fact is a conviction that a significant number of people hold to be true based on extensive evidence. Philosophically, a fact is a unit of being, capable of bearing meaning, and that meaning becomes clear when the propensity of the facts point to a logical conclusion. The facts are just facts until they are united and fit together to form meaning.

Pause and Reflect

What are some differences between your organization's core values and its vision and strategy? Is there a difference between a key value and a principle?

Why is it important that your organization has constant values? Does that mean those values should never change?

Why is it important that you possess passionate values?

Is it important that your values be biblical? Why?

Identify some ways that central beliefs drive your business or organization.

Strategic Planning

Centuries ago, the writer of Proverbs observed: "Any enterprise is built by wise planning, becomes strong through common sense and profits wonderfully by keeping abreast of the facts" (Proverbs 24:3-4 TLB).

Most leaders agree that planning is an important part of the leadership picture. However, when it comes to actually doing the planning or scheduling time for effective planning, most leaders also agree that they fail in this area. Leaders I have surveyed indicate their planning process is hindered by the lack of a system or format to follow. Many also confess they have never actually been intimately involved in such a process. Most of the planning they have done was intuitive or hunch-driven. The "seat of the pants" approach can work for some who are very insightful and well informed about the landscape of their industry. For most leaders, however, there is a clear need for a better understanding of planning – the purpose, process, and expected results.

The Christian leader's planning process is unique in that it starts with the realization that God has a plan and a purpose for the Christian organization and its people. For example, Jeremiah 29:11 states: "For I know the plans I have for you, declares the Lord, plans to prosper you and not to harm you, plans to give you a hope and a future." Additionally, in Psalm 32:8 God says: "I will instruct you and teach you in the way you should go; I will counsel you and watch over you." In these and many other verses, God makes it clear that planning is part of His very nature. For Christian leaders, the first step in the planning process is to recognize the fact that we need to seek God's guidance. Our job is to determine the actions God wants us to take and then trust God for the results. The Scripture declares, "Many are the plans in a man's heart, but it is the Lord's purpose that prevails" (Proverbs 19:21).

Planning is both a creative and a critical thinking process. The creative thinking side is accomplished by when we explore new territories, open the windows of our minds to new and fresh possibilities and are willing to test the new ideas in the practical world of daily business. The critical thinking side comes into play when we systematically develop the strategies by which to accomplish the dream and establish a set of criteria by which the new ideas will be evaluated.

The actual process begins with identifying the overall purpose of the project and then to identify the activities to be performed, the sequence of those activities and the resources required. It involves asking these "why" questions:

1. Why is this important?
2. Why should I get involved?
3. Why do we need to have these things done?
4. Why should this be a top priority?

Once these starting questions have been explored and answered, the planning process has begun.

As mentioned earlier, one of my favorite portions of the Bible is the Old Testament book of Nehemiah. Nehemiah was a layman and a business leader in the time of a powerful Middle Eastern ruler; initially serving as a slave and later to be given a political post. What we learn from his writing is not only spiritually helpful but also provides a wealth of leadership and management wisdom. One example of this is when Nehemiah articulates the reasons for rebuilding the wall around Jerusalem to his co-workers. "You see the trouble we are in. Jerusalem lies in ruins and its gates have been burned with fire. Come, let us rebuild the wall of Jerusalem and we will no longer be in disgrace" (Nehemiah 2:17).

Another example of planning is recorded in Genesis 6:19-22. In this passage, God asks Noah to build the ark and then explains His purpose to him.

While planning can be an exciting and future-oriented process, it is also hard work and can be discouraging. It is time consuming to develop a good plan and in the meantime many will likely ask, "What are you doing with all the time you are spending on this project?" That is why planning is often put off. To be sure you are on the right track and can be productive in the process, some basic steps need to be implemented to make sure you have a workable plan.

First, develop a vision of the completed plan. The vision is a mental image of the completed plan that should stimulate action, spark innovation and prompt creativity. Like the purpose or cause, a vision motivates people to make a strong commitment to the project. It also helps develop unity and personal conviction and justifies the expenditure of resources. Visualizing the end result, just like establishing a vision for the organization, helps determine the steps needed for accomplishing the plan.

Second, develop objectives you can measure along the way. A measurable objective tells exactly what will be accomplished, how much is to be accomplished and when it will be completed. It is important to keep in mind that the objective must be manageable or controllable. Before the rebuilding of the wall of Jerusalem, King

Artaxerxes asked Nehemiah two important questions that required the formation of measurable objectives. The first (2:4) was, "What do you want?" The second (2:6) was, "How long will your journey take?" These questions help clarify the objectives in terms of questions like what, how much and when. In other words, the objectives became measurable.

Recognize that measurable objectives will give meaning to your dreams for a better process, product, or service. Without measurable objectives people tend to talk and plan in generalities. Measurable objectives, on the other hand, help people know what to look and work for as the days unfold. This can also apply to matters of faith like prayer for when we are more specific in prayer we can better know when God answers.

A third step is to develop valid and worthy objectives. A good objective is defined as one that can be accomplished. Every objective or target should be established so that it is within the realm of possibility for it to be accomplished. If it is beyond their reach, people will become discouraged or lose interest. An objective must be realistic. It is something that the organization really needs to accomplish. It has to be compatible with other organizational objectives and goals. Each objective within the organization should contribute to the overall purpose or cause of the organization. A good objective is always motivational. Good objectives stimulate interest and commitment. Good objectives also provide a spark that ignites people to action. It is something that will draw them forward and upward. By taking these things into consideration, you will be on your way to effectively leading your team in a profitable planning experience.

Once you have identified all the activities needed in the plan, the next thing is to place them in a proper sequence or order. The right activity performed at the wrong time can create problems in the process. Identifying the activities describes how the plan will be carried out. Placing the activity in proper sequence tells us where it fits in the events. You need also to consider all the resources that are needed like people, space, equipment, supplies, time, money and more.

In reviewing the process we can summarize six basic stages in the planning process:

Step One. Identify the purpose of the project or activity. The purpose tells why the plan is important. The purpose develops conviction and commitment.

Step Two. Visualize the plan completed. By doing this you begin to build confidence in the project and it can help speed up the planning process.

Step Three. Develop measurable objectives. Objectives tell what will be accomplished, how much will be accomplished and when.

Step Four. Identify the activities needed to accomplish the objectives. Activities explain how the objectives will be achieved. This phase of planning should focus on the participation, innovation and creativity of your planning team.

Step Five. Place the activities in proper sequence. This step will establish where each activity fits into the overall plan.

Step Six. Determine the resources needed to achieve the plan. Look at people, space, equipment, supplies, time and money. The extent of resources needed will depend on the activities to be performed and their sequence. This budgeting step must be carefully done and the information made available to all involved.

Strategic planning is really a process of thinking and acting; it is "strategic thinking." The thinking part is probably the most important part of the process. As one author said in a bit of an exaggeration, "Thinking is everything. Planning is nothing." Often companies make the mistake of hiring a consultant to help them develop a plan; the work gets done, a planning document is completed, but the plan is put in a notebook on the shelf and never visited again. Planning must be an ongoing process because change is constant and with every change the plan must adapt. If not reviewed on a regular and systematic basis, plans quickly become obsolete. A good planning process also helps the company stay alert to changes locally, regionally, and nationally that can impact effectiveness, morale, and especially the bottom line.

Principles of Planning

A few fundamental planning principles need to be identified so that the leader can professionally guide the process. They are as follows:

1. The higher the level where planning takes place in the company, the broader the scope.
2. The longer the time frame projected for the plan, the more flexibility is required in the plan.
3. Current decisions made during the planning process will limit future choices.
4. The more attention that is systematically given to the implementation of a plan, the greater is the possibility of it being properly accomplished.
5. Effort applied to the accomplishment of a plan should be commensurate with the results expected.
6. In the new plan, the greater the departure from the way things have been done in the past, the greater will be the resistance to the plan.
7. The clearer and more tangible the targets identified in the new plan, the greater the likelihood of significant effort being applied to their successful completion.

Taking each principle in turn and helping your team understand and apply them to the systematic planning process will greatly enrich the experience.

First, top levels of management from the board of directors through the executives of the company need to endorse the plan.

They have the responsibility to ensure that plans are realizable, have broad input from appropriate sources within the firm, are made available and regularly updated and have appropriate resources dedicated to the project.

Next, the length of the plan will affect the expected results. Short range plans need to be consistent and coordinated with long range plans. The degree of flexibility required in the plan should be monitored by the leadership to insure that the plan will stay on target. Be a good steward of the plan entrusted to your care and regularly report on progress. How money is spent for manpower, materials, facilities and equipment and what results are being achieved should be identified.

Third, current decisions have an enormous effect upon any future decisions made in the company. Care must be taken to examine the potential impact of any significant decisions in the planning process. The "what if" question should be regularly asked and answered with the best available data possible.

Fourth, is the generally accepted truth that you must put in a positive effort and consistently monitor the progress, if you want positive results. A college coach once coined the expression, "You can only expect what you regularly inspect." This applies to the planning process as well. Unless the team knows that there is consistent follow-up and that there are high standards of expectation in the execution of responsibilities, you will not be able to expect high quality results. Effective employees want to know what is expected and take pride in doing a quality job. When they know someone is taking notice it is even better.

Fifth, relates to the expression originating in the beginning of the computer age: "Garbage in, garbage out." In other words, the investment you make in the process will determine to a large degree what the results will be. As my wife would say to her piano students many years ago, "It is not practice that makes perfect; it is only perfect practice that makes perfect." Too often we are satisfied with busyness and do not check productivity.

Sixth, when it comes to change most people have some level of built-in resistance. Change is a good thing, but people need to be prepared for change and every planning process introduces change! The greater the change, the greater will be the natural resistance. Planned change, by taking measured steps and giving people sufficient time to make the adjustment, is usually best, although no one way fits all situations.

Finally, when most people are able to see the steps in the plan in clear and tangible ways, they will generally come to accept new ideas and participate in the ongoing development of the venture. I was once told that what a leader talks about, dreams about, prays about, prioritizes and works at steadily in his or her life will normally come to pass. My experience over the years has confirmed that concept. I can also testify to the fact that things always took longer than I expected and answers to difficult situations often came from unexpected sources. Yet most of the best things I learned in life came out of difficulties, not out of blessings. The comfort I have had over the years is that as a Christian, I knew that the Lord was on my side and that eternity would reveal the true picture. Serving the Lord by helping those around me and being grateful for every day and every opportunity, has helped me along the way. While it is comforting to know that God is a forgiving God, make sure that your plans do not violate God's principles.

Pause and Reflect

Review your organization's planning strategy and timetable. Have a planning specialist review your planning process and existing documents and present a plan for planning. Set aside some defined quality time each month for top leaders to get together to review progress of the existing plans. Commit to being a company that plans its future and then pursues its plans.

CHAPTER 3

LEADERSHIP POTHOLES AND PITFALLS

HAVE you ever been faced with a problem that you thought was totally unique to your leadership experience? Scores of leaders every day face issues that seem challenging, unusual and somewhat unsolvable. But wise is the leader that recognizes the valuable, collective wisdom of those who have gone before.

King Solomon, the wisest man to have ever lived, observed there is nothing new under the sun (Ecclesiastes 1:9) and so is it not more valuable to learn from the mistakes of others than to make those same mistakes yourself? Consider the counsel of prior leaders and authors as you read their books and resources. It is far superior to learn best practices and the right way to do things by reading what others have written, rather than to stumble along trying to uncover good answers while still searching for the right questions.

Learn to read rapidly so you can absorb the most you can out of the wide selection of quality leadership literature. As you read this chapter make a list of the challenges you have yet to face so that surprises in the future will be minimized.

The Pitfall of Misperception

One foundational issue to good leadership is the relationship between authority and submission. No leader worth his or her salt can be successful over the long haul unless they have lived both as a follower and a leader and know how to be both. It sounds like a contradiction in terms but a good leader is also a good follower. Winston Churchill is reported to have observed, "Courage is what it takes to stand up and speak. Courage is also what it takes to sit down and listen." Leadership and followership are two sides of the same coin.

To clarify this it is important to understand and properly distinguish between authority and submission. It is like knowing when to talk and when to remain silent. A wise leader once told me in jest that is better to keep quiet and let people think you are ignorant than to open your mouth and remove all doubt. It is the same with authority and submission. They are complimentary concepts and knowing when to use each of them is important.

This is illustrated in the life of the Lord Jesus Christ. He set the pattern by His death, which was the ultimate submission and by His resurrection which was the ultimate authority. In the fast-paced world of life and business, these two types of experiences can quickly come upon you and you have to make a quick decision as to the proper and best role to take in light of the situation.

Perhaps a look at how this was faced by a leader in ancient times will help clarify the issue. The Apostle Paul was originally named for the first political leader of Israel, King Saul. Saul turned out to be a rebel king, one that mirrored the nation rather than led the nation. In the New Testament, Saul encounters Jesus Christ on the Damascus Road. As a result of this life changing experience, God changed his name from Saul to Paul. The difference was a change in character and style. He went from Saul, the mighty, to Paul, a name meaning small or little. His power now came, not from stature or physical strength like his namesake, but rather from humility and "almighty meekness." Leading from motives of personal vanity is one step down the road to failure; instead, lead with a heart of humility and a commitment to the welfare of others.

I remember how easy it is, in the early days of a leader's experience, to take things personally. It seems that a person tends to exert their authority more readily when their experience base is limited. It is a way of justifying their position when they do not know what else to do. This is further complicated by the fact that we often assume that the actions and responses of others are most likely directed exclusively at us. To overcome this we need to learn that humility, submission and objectivity are tremendous assets for the leader who is in the first few years of the leadership journey. There are many more lessons to be learned along the way but, as the old expression goes, "well begun, half done."

Leaders often wonder, "What about my authority? How can I lead if people don't recognize my authority?" We need to recognize that authority arrives in two interrelated ways. First, other people give it to you. Sometimes you have authority in a physical sense, as when your children are born. Sometimes you have political authority if you are elected to an office or position. Sometimes you have economical authority, when you receive a paycheck. Authority comes to you from others accepting the fact that you have it. Anyone with some type of title has a measure of authority.

The other way authority arrives is from God. Christians often do not realize that God gives authority to each one of His children. It is legitimate, latent, potential, inherent and true authority – and God gives it to you whether others accept it or not. It is our responsibility to assert the authority Christ has given us, but how we do it is very important. This type of authority is usually discovered when other people observe your exercise of both your natural and spiritual gifts. When you do what your good at and encourage others to do what they are good at, your leadership ability begins to take shape and others will see it. Whether others accept it or not is their responsibility, not ours. Both the authority others give you as well as the authority God provides are ultimately both from Him. How we use that authority can either be strength or a significant weakness.

It is important now to address the fact, faith and feeling issue. As human beings we are strongly influenced by the emotions that swirl within us. Leaders are not immune from this and in fact, may find that this is one of the most difficult leadership problems for them to objectively face. The Bible records numerous examples of how this dilemma caused problems for leaders. The first king of Israel demonstrated in his lifetime how difficult an issue this was for him. His emotions and mental state seemed to constantly conflict with the facts and faith.

The best example of how this was designed to work was demonstrated in the resurrection of Christ. There the ultimate demonstration of submission was the surrendering of the Son's will to that of the Father. In the matter of our faith, this is the example we follow. We choose to surrender our will to His so it becomes, "not my will but yours be done." Both the intellect and the emotions are governed by the will. Christ seeks my will; when that issue has been settled the intellectual and emotional problems can be resolved. The Lord never "forces" us to believe or coerces us into faith. He may create circumstances around us to cause us to seek answers from Him, but He will always wait for us to open our hearts to Him.

In the end it comes down to a willingness on your part to desire to do the will of God. When a leader submits to the authority of God and seeks guidance through prayer, study of the Scriptures and the counsel of godly friends, God will ultimately provide the direction. Time is not the issue. From experience I can say that God has His own schedule and generally stretches me way beyond my comfort zone. The sooner a believer learns this, the easier is the road.

Facts first, then faith and finally feelings; this is the unchanging sequence. The most important point to remember is that your will ultimately determines the meaning of the facts. Facts are units of information, capable of bearing meaning, but a fact is only a fact and until the facts fit together into some intelligible pattern, they remain isolated bits of information.

It is vital for a Christian leader in any walk of life, to maintain a personal, daily and vibrant spiritual life. God's plan for us is that we continue to grow and develop. Any type of stagnation is really regression. The fact that God has given you a leadership opportunity is an act of grace. Using your leadership privilege for the glory of God and the good of those around you is an act of love.

Pause and Reflect

What types of issues are you currently facing? Who in your circle of family, friends or colleagues can be of most help in giving you perspective and direction? Talk with the friend who has the best reputation for positive thought and spiritual insight and share your life and dreams. It may also be profitable to make a list of the top five tough decisions that you are currently facing that need to be given to God in prayer. Then give God time to work out some solutions while you continue to wait on Him in prayer.

The Pitfall of Pride

Pride can be viewed in either a good or bad sense. It is good to take a measure of pride in our work, meaning we should invest ourselves fully in the tasks before us so whatever we do in word or deed brings glory to God and benefit to God's people. The negative side of pride is when we take credit ourselves for what God has given to us. The opposite of pride is humility, to bow down or to serve and help someone else. Most leaders grapple with the issue of pride at some time in their lives.

One of the persistent prayers that Dr. Billy Graham has referred to in his life is the prayer that God would keep him from a proud heart and spirit. William Sloan Coffin also said it well when he wrote, "There is no smaller package in the world than a man wrapped up in himself."[9]

Closely related to the issue of pride is the characteristic known as ambition. Is all ambition warranted or unwarranted? When can ambition become a detriment rather than an advantage to the leader? The answer probably lies in the source and direction of the

---

9 As cited by Gregory K. Morris, Ph.D., *In Pursuit of Leadership: Principles and Practices from the Life of Moses* (Longwood, FL: Xulon Press, 2006) p. 211.

ambition. If it is self centered and self promoting it is most likely a negative thing. If it springs from a desire to help others, please God and promote a positive and worthwhile vision and mission, then it is most likely is a good thing. Just seizing the initiative and moving forward with blind ambition can be a dangerous and negative path. Calvin Miller once wrote, "Careers, even religious careers, may become little more than forums of our own advancement. But how are we to deal with such ambition? Our longing after Christ must exceed our need for status in the world."[10]

A Biblical Perspective

A Christian leader needs some assurance from the Lord that the goals and dreams they are pursuing are spiritually correct and can be productive for all concerned. Seek solid evidence that the Lord has been opening up this particular opportunity and will be honored through it. Consider King Solomon's reaction to the circumstances surrounding his ascension to the kingship and God's gifting to him for the exercise of leadership (1 Kings 1:3). What he did highlights the need for decisive action that is consistent with divine calling.

When you observe prospective leaders, look at whether or not there is a demonstration of responsible action in tasks previously undertaken. What is that individual's orientation toward ministry and service? What is his or her desire for those who are under his care and direction? When ambition misdirects glory and praise to the leader rather than to the Lord, ambition can lead to disaster.

Jesus Christ, the master leader, was a master strategist. Being God in the flesh, even while He laid aside His prerogatives as God in order to minister and give His life a ransom for many, He still remained gifted with the all the qualities and insights that great leaders have and demonstrated them throughout His relatively short leadership on earth. Planning, leading organizing, supervising, directing, communicating, controlling and correcting were among the scores

---

10 Calvin Miller, *A Hunger for the Holy: Nurturing Intimacy with Christ* (West Monroe, LA: Howard Publishing Co., 2003) pp. 45-46.

of leadership and management skills and activities He demonstrated repeatedly during those three years of ministry.

Jesus had access to all power at all times, as clearly noted by Satan during the interchange we call the Temptation (Matthew 4:1-11). The conversation between Satan and Jesus illustrated Christ's tough-mindedness and a clear focus on His mission and values. Three all-encompassing challenges to His life and purpose were met with Scriptural responses and steely resolve to do what was right regardless of the difficulty. Jesus rejected three unrighteous strategies that Satan proposed and in response stated His kingdom-building guidelines. While the challenges presented by Satan had some arguable merit on the surface, Jesus saw through the arguments, understood the end results from such a course of action and rejected the challenges as being easily corruptible goals.

The Power of Influence

One author, writing about these temptations from a leadership perspective, described them as the seduction of pleasure, power and parade. These are three types of temptations that can come upon a leader in a subtle and insidious manner. Good leaders, even apparently humble leaders, have been seduced over time as their reputation for being effective and successful has grown. Their ability to influence wealthy and powerful people to support their endeavor or cause has sometimes brought with it the compelling need for continued and ever-increasing success. As a result, some have taken shortcuts to achieve immediate satisfaction, achievements or recognition. This is a dangerous path which will eventually lead to failure.

Another issue arises when the leader becomes "appetite driven." In this case the leader becomes prosperity and pleasure oriented. Both of these targets are self-serving and potentially dangerous. God does not condemn prosperity, but He wants His children to be disciplined. He warns us that the power of the purse can corrupt our lives. While God also promises pleasures, He reminds us that our primary purpose is not selfish personal enrichment and gratification;

but is selfless service to others and the glorification of His name. Service is the higher value. Prosperity and pleasure are lesser values subject to the higher.

I have had the privilege of being involved in fundraising for several Christian and community organizations. As a fundraiser I have learned some marvelous lessons, both positive and negative. I have met people who are self-centered and want to hold tight to what they have, but I also met some very wonderful people. Then there were the "wait and see" folks – and if my experience is any accurate measure of this topic I believe that those types of people will be forever waiting to see! They wait to see if they will get the money from somewhere to give, but they never do. They wait to see until they have accumulated enough to care for their lifetime needs and those of their extended family – they never do. They wait to see if the organization will do exactly what they want it to do – it never does and they never give. Learning not to take rejection personally and leaving these folks with the Lord is the only sane way to live.

Have you ever noticed that some people seem to have the "gift of giving?" They are good stewards of the resources God has entrusted to their care. Their attitude encourages others and is demonstrated in their pattern of giving. They believe that what they have accumulated is all from the Lord and that in reality He owns it all. They want to be good managers of the resources and give a good account of the things God has put in their control. They maintain a biblical pattern of faithful giving to their local church and legitimate ministries that provide help to believers first, and then, as the Bible says, to all men. They have a plan for giving and base that plan on what the Bible teaches. They follow New Testament guidelines for charitable giving and, in fact, love to give. They also recognize that money is a representation of power. In the business world they choose to give power to others via company policies that provide fair wages and benefits and by their charitable support of appropriate causes.

Pause and Reflect

God has blessed you with talents, skills and abilities. Which ones do you consider your best and greatest strengths? How are you using them for others? Describe the results you have you in the past from these abilities.

What are your weaknesses? Who do you have on your team to complement you and bring strength where you are weak?

Pray for continued humility and honesty in all your endeavors and relationships. Be a real, genuine and giving leader who enriches and enables those around you to fulfill their potentials. Do not be a "people-user," but rather strive to be a "people builder."

The Pitfall of Time

Time is a precious resource, given to us by God. It is graciously distributed in equal amounts (24 hours in a day), one day at a time. An indication of a good and productive leader is the successful use of the time God has entrusted to your care. Leaders who inspire followers to dedicate themselves to achieve the highest goals also care for their followers by protecting their investment of time, realizing that time is like money and both are gifts from God. Leaders who allow followers to become so involved in their work that personal life and family suffer are not doing what God desires.

Leaders sometimes set the pace for others by the work they do and the hours they put in, not realizing what they consider "normal" is probably not the best pattern for the rest of the team. Some time ago I had a subordinate tell me that he worked long hours because he had seen me do it years earlier and thought that was the way to be successful. What he did not know was the pattern of work he observed those many years ago was *not* something to be emulated. I had neglected some of the important things in my life for the urgent things and had to make significant changes or suffer significant loss. Fortunately, I learned my lesson before the damage was irreparable.

Because time is so important there is a temptation to take short-cuts. We need to learn to work smarter, not harder. That does not mean, however, that we should look for shortcuts to doing things the best possible way. In fact, it might mean just the opposite.

William Cary was a missionary to Africa in the early days of the modern missionary period. He was a man of direction, discipline and divine encouragement, far removed from the leaders who seek self-gratification and self glorification. He was a self confessed "plodder." He was thorough, careful and dedicated but not known as a "flashy, quick leader." He was the opposite of the leader who takes shortcuts. His biography shows that he would often take the slower route to the goal rather than the shortest route, but he was a finisher. His reputation and record of service spoke volumes and as leaders have said over the years, it is not how you start the race that counts, it is how you finish. Leaders need to be finishers.

It is in the little things of leadership that the big mistakes and brilliant moves are made. Most leaders are rarely tempted to compromise with evil in order to reach their goals, although the occasions are there. Too often, misguided leaders accept the popular idea that success is only possible by taking shortcuts. It is the old philosophical argument that the end justifies the means. This attitude can bless any tactic as acceptable as long as the outcome can be described as successful or profitable and even sometimes is deemed to be moral. But moral goals cannot be reached by immoral means; success and profits are not the legitimate result of illegal, immoral and unethical behavior. Once the leader succumbs to this errant philosophy, the enterprise is being set up for future failure. The old saying, "the truth will win out" will be validated in time.

Leaders like to be liked; which is what all of us desire if we are completely honest with ourselves. But to be liked at any cost is self defeating. As Matthew 4:1-11 indicates, Christ's third temptation was an attempt to seduce Him into taking the shortcut of parade and sensationalism. In his final attempt to ensnare Jesus, the Devil promised to get Him on the ancient equivalent of the six o'clock news. He painted the scenario of Jesus standing on the brink of the temple and diving off, only to be caught inches before the ground by angels with a heavenly safety net. Recognition, headlines and center stage are addictive allures for a leader. It is nice to be appreciated and to receive that recognition in a very public way is especially addictive. A cynical politician once claimed that leadership was simply finding a parade and getting in front of it. He didn't care what the cause was as long as he was going to be at the front of the line and asked to make the speeches. This is another pitfall for leaders.

Maintaining a humble and servant type of perspective is the only way to avoid these subtle attacks on the integrity of leadership. The memorable Lord Acton observed that power tends to corrupt and absolute power tends to corrupts absolutely. To this reflection can be added the corollary that human life is a strange tale of three things: securing power, maintaining power and losing power. Many have addressed this issue down through the years but it remains a significant threat to godly, successful and effective leadership. It is a danger that wise leaders seek to avoid at all costs. This is complicated by insecure followers who do not respond well to the stress they feel from effective leaders in power positions. Insecure people, who find themselves faced with a powerful leader and therefore experience stress, may act as though they have no power, or may face a pervading sense of powerlessness. In so doing, they deny the use of the power God has given them for both living and service. Also, many people who respond this way tend to meet every pressing need by their own effort and in their own strength in an attempt to solve issues rather than trusting the Lord to see them safely through the immediate circumstance.

That is to say, the manager does not use the alternative of "brute, absolute" power but rather the kind of authority that is exercised *by* others, rather than *over* others. The principle-centered leader believes that his power, used wisely, will cause others to have more power. The end result will be that the leader is also enriched with power. Integrative power is principle-based. It is found in principle-centered and integrated power. This is not the kind of power that a manager uses capriciously or by whim. Rather he or she follows a set of effective and clearly communicated principles in carrying out managerial duties. This is the type of leadership that students in various levels of the educational spectrum often experience with a highly respected and beloved teacher. The results of principle-centered power is that mutual commitment and respect for one another grows continuously and will be marked by quality, distinction and excellence in organizational processes, relationships and activities.

Dr. Stephen R. Covey in his book *Principled-Centered Leadership*[11] stresses matters such as:

- *Persuasion* which includes sharing reasons and rationale; making a strong case for your position while maintaining genuine respect for the ideas and perspectives of others.
- *Patience* with the process and the person. In spite of the failings, shortcomings or inconveniences created by others as well as your own impatience for the achievement of goals; this leader maintains a long-term perspective and continues to stay committed to the objectives, despite obstacles and resistance.
- *Gentleness* which is not harshness, hardness or forcefulness, when dealing with the vulnerabilities, disclosures and feelings people might express.
- *Teachableness* which means operating with the assumption that you do not have all the answers or insights and that you value different viewpoints, judgments and experiences.
- *Acceptance* by withholding judgment, giving benefit of doubt, requiring no evidence or special performance as a condition for your acceptance.
- *Kindness* or being sensitive, caring, thoughtful and remembering to do the little things which are so important in a relationship.
- *Openness*, by acquiring accurate information and perspectives about persons, holding each one in high regard, regardless of what they own, control or do.

---

11 Stephen R. Covey, *Principled-Centered Leadership* (New York: Fireside Press, 1992) 336 pp.

- *Compassion and confrontation* which is acknowledging error, mistakes and the need to make "course corrections" in a context of genuine care, concern and warmth, making it safe for people to take a risk.
- *Consistency* which is guarding against the use of your leadership as a manipulative tool when you do not get your way or when you feel trapped.
- *Integrity* which is honestly matching words and feelings with thoughts and actions; with no desire other than the good of others; without malice or deceit; without taking advantage, manipulation, or control; constantly reviewing your intent as you strive for congruence.

Pause and Reflect

Are you a people-grower or people-hinderer? What have you done in recent months to mentor and develop a subordinate? In what specific ways have you exemplified some of the characteristics to which Covey refers? Do you tend to seize or abdicate power? How does your tendency affect your direct reports? What type of power are you comfortable with and do you use regularly?

It is important to remember that insecure people who find themselves faced with a powerful leader may experience stress, and therefore act as though they have no power due to a pervading sense of powerlessness. Unfortunately, in so doing, they deny the use of the power God has given them for both living and service. Also, many people who respond in this manner tend to meet every pressing need by their own effort and in their own strength in an attempt to be relevant rather than trusting the Lord to see them through the immediate circumstance. Review your executive team members to insure that they are all comfortable with your leadership style. If they are not, there will be lingering resentment that will hinder effective team productivity.

The Pitfall of Passion

The pitfall of passion is not the most inspiring topic for leaders to address, but since opportunities for sexual temptation are so prevalent it must be faced.

The Bible speaks with clarity and force on this topic. In the book that bears his name, the prophet Malachi writes:

> Another thing you do: you flood the Lord's altar with tears. You weep and wail because he no longer pays attention to your offerings or accepts them with pleasure at your hands. You ask, 'Why?' Is it because the Lord is acting as a witness between you and the wife of your youth, because you have broken faith with her, though she is your partner, the wife of your marriage covenant? Has not the Lord made them one? In flesh and spirit they are his. And why one? Because he was seeking godly offspring. So guard yourself in your spirit, and do not break faith with the wife of your youth.
>
> – Malachi 2.13-16

Sexual impurity is a subtle and persistent problem in today's world. My experience tells me that even the church has taken a much softer approach to sexual sins with the passing of time. Current numbers indicate that there is no statistical difference between churched and unchurched people when it comes to unfaithfulness, divorce and remarriage. The office, the schoolroom, the church, the service club, in fact, every place where there is a gathering of people, Satan may use as an opportunity to corrupt.

Recognizable patterns of behavior are evident. Illicit relationships begin with a) conversation and light intimate talk, b) progress to initiating a personal relationship (is the person approachable, available, and agreeable), c) establish physical closeness, d) move to involve fantasy and rationalization of wrong actions and ultimately, e) lead to sexual activity. While the pattern may be the same, the settings are all different. In this subtle way, the Devil gains the advantage. Natural human drives, if undisciplined and uncontrolled by the Holy Spirit, make us ripe for a fall in our sexually saturated culture.

At first blush (and I use the word loosely, for there is little shame in today's world), the initial feelings that come from such a relationship always appear to be positive. People seem to be happier than they have ever been before, more alive, more sensitive, more creative and even more passionate. As the imagination begins to work, the thought life develops scenarios of bliss, ignoring both the warnings in the Word of God and the reality of the tragedy about to unfold.

Even if the affair does not blossom into a full blown sexual encounter in physical adultery, it may be "spiritual adultery." This has been defined as the unintentional entering into another's heart that easily occurs between trusting people who spend time together. The Lord's warning through Malachi to "guard our spirits" is one to be taken seriously. We can make idols in our lives out of a variety of things and one of them is "feeling loved." Being appreciated, being needed, being respected, being recognized for competence and other similar needs can also become idols which passion can take to the extreme and lead us away from purity and proper innocence.

Devoting time to the open and honest discussion of sexual immorality and the need for sexual purity is becoming increasingly important in our day and age. While lying, pride, greed, stealing, etc. are all evil in God's sight, there is a sense in which sexual sins are in a different class from other sins. The lingering effects of this sin in a person's memory can create persistent turmoil in their life.

Paul makes an issue of sexual sin as a special category. "Run away from sexual sin! No other sin so clearly affects the body as this one does. For sexual immorality is a sin against your own body. Or don't you know that your body is the temple of the Holy Spirit, who lives in you and was given to you by God?" (1 Corinthians 6:18-19).

The church at Corinth had a particular problem. The city had a reputation for sexual excess; in fact, in Paul's day a euphemism for prostitutes was "the Corinthian girl." There was a high hill near Corinth topped with an acropolis which was a temple for prostitution and idol worship. It is said that the women had arrows carved into the bottom of their shoes so their footprints would leave a trail for men to follow them up to the temple for sexual activity.

Sexual temptation in our society is prevalent and growing exponentially. We are offered a sexual smorgasbord on the internet, on television and even in schools as condoms are distributed. Abstinence is ridiculed in the media and by many health providers and educators. One writer says that "sexual purity stands as one of the great defining characteristics of a faithful child of God. Yet many Christians struggle to remain sexually pure."

Christian leaders in all walks of life at all levels of society must commit to living purely and leading righteously as the spiritual and moral decline of our culture intensifies. Here are some practical ways for us to evaluate our risks and "guard our spirits."

1. Do you struggle with pornography? What types of magazines and movies are you reading and watching? Would you be embarrassed to have Jesus sit beside you while you read, watch TV, work at your computer, or attend a movie? Avoid any magazines, television programs, computer sites or movies that cannot pass the Jesus test. This will take discipline and courage but good leaders have both.

2. Are you experiencing persistent sexual temptations? What specifically can you do to conquer this problem? Seek out a mature leader who you can trust, who has a good reputation, who is grounded in Christian truth and ask that person to hold you accountable in this area.

3. Are you guilty of past sexual immorality? If so, have you confessed your sin to God? Reinforce that decision and confession by making a specific commitment to live the rest of your life in sexual purity.

4. Memorize 1 Corinthians 6:18 and ask God to give you the ability to flee all sexual immorality from this point on.

While this is a sensitive and difficult issue to discuss, it is noteworthy that in the Old Testament there are only six capital offenses

– that is, six crimes for which people were condemned to death by stoning. Two of those crimes were sexual sins.

We tend to segregate sins into those that only affect you and those that can affect others. However, sin is so pervasive that its tentacles always seek others to involve and destroy. In the New Testament there are numerous references to sexual purity and the condemnation of sexual sin. In fact, nowhere in the Bible did God require death for liars or truce-breakers, but he did require execution for those who had sexual involvement with people other than their marriage partners.

The sexual revolution sought to replace the traditional emphasis on sexual self-restraint with an emphasis on sexual freedom. It promoted the idea that people should be free to make love with whomever they wished without the constriction of marriage (a monogamous, public, legally binding commitment). It promised greater happiness, but now as we look back almost five decades later, it is clear that our world suffers from a plague of problems stemming from the abandonment of traditional norms of sexual morality.

For any Christian, sexual purity and commitment to the biblical ideal of marriage is non-negotiable. Malachi explains that the Lord is seeking godly offspring, so teach your children, grandchildren and great grandchildren what God's standard is along with His plan for life and relationships. Leaders, be an example of a true believer; live purely, productively, purposefully and powerfully for the glory of God and the good of those you love.

Pause and Reflect

In what areas of your business and private life are you most vulnerable to sexual temptation? What have you done in terms of communicating your convictions, scheduling your time appropriately and controlling your physical environment to avoid temptation?

Recruit some key praying friends to pray for you daily and review the Scriptures that speak to purity of heart, mind and body. Determine to practice godly living and flee "youthful lusts." Do not put yourself in situations where the only barrier between you and temptation is your own self control!

The Pitfall of Anger

It comes in many shapes and intensities, but we all have it. Anger is a common pitfall for leaders. The more responsible your position, the more insight you have into the workings of your organization, the more you come to know about the people you work with, the greater the potential for some level of anger! It has been my observation as a leader that people with anger issues quite often will accuse others of the very problem they have.

Some people have dispositions that are calm and generally well controlled. Others have personalities and a history of behavior that are better described as volatile. For the Christian leader, it is important to control your emotions and be skilled in diffusing situations where emotions run strong.

Many people are raised with the idea that a good offense is the best defense. They will generally begin to address a problem situation with a display of anger. Historian Arthur M. Schlesinger wrote that President Andrew Jackson deliberately made people believe he was angry in order to scare them off.[12] He chose the appearance of anger, acting in a furious, intimidating manner as his way of scaring off his critics. It is said that when they left, he would coolly light his pipe and chuckle over the fact that they thought he was angry.

Anger is something everyone faces from time to time, but some handle it better than others. It often arises from fear, guilt or hurt. The Bible recognizes that anger is part of the human experience when it counsels, "Be angry but do not sin." This command points to the responsibility of controlling personal impulses. Anger uncontrolled is debilitating. It saps your energy, overloads and confuses your mind and distracts you from discovering the best resolution. In fact, unresolved anger will distort your perception of people. It

---

12 Arthur M. Schlesinger, Jr., *The Age of Jackson* (New York: New American Library, 1949) p. 32.

takes away your ability to understand the intricacies of issues and the paths to conflict resolution. In fact, others will detect our residual anger, despite our best efforts to camouflage it. Like it or not, a careless word here or a facial reaction there will reveal our true inner selves.

Unresolved anger invites stress, depression, disappointment and a continuing lack of satisfaction with our work. It must be properly resolved or it will negatively affect our personal performance, the work of our colleagues and the productivity of our enterprise. Resolving anger may necessitate one or more of the following tactics:

- A cathartic approach where people work out their anger in a safe and protected environment with or without professional help.
- A reflective approach where rationality and an honest review of all the facts and opinions are brought to the level of conscious decision-making.
- A spiritual approach where the leader realizes that the anger has more to do with his or her spiritual condition than emotional or cognitive process.

Whatever the source, anger must be confronted and resolved otherwise the leader, followers and the organization will suffer. According to the Scriptures, anger can arise without premeditation yet it can be controlled if faced honestly, openly and with persistent reliance on the Holy Spirit of God, who is the true counselor, teacher and friend. The sooner the problem is addressed, the faster will be the resolution.

Pause and Reflect

Remember that the Bible commands, "Be angry and sin not." Anger is an emotion that can spring up quickly for both good and bad reasons. How you handle it is key.

Review the relationships, activities and situations that have produced some degree of anger in the recent past. Pray for forgiveness and plan for a more peaceful response in future situations. Become aware of the settings and the people who cause your emotions to rise. Approach them in the future with wisdom and control.

The Pitfall of Careless Talk

Leaders face many, many challenges, but one of the greatest is the uncontrolled and perverse use of the tongue. While the term "perversion" is typically associated with sexual sins, a more subtle and perhaps more dangerous perversion is the use of the tongue. We are warned in Scripture by James that "no one can tame the tongue." To make matters worse, he goes on to say the tongue is "set on fire by hell."

The third chapter of James contains numerous ideas and principles that Christian leaders need to absorb. First, James 3:2 states the wise and accountable leader realizes that by paying careful attention to what comes out of their mouth they are demonstrating maturity and wisdom. James says that an individual who is "perfect," meaning complete and mature, is very careful with what they say. Careful, well thought out speech is a sign of maturity.

Second, James 3:3-4 continues the theme with a comparison. Horses and ships are controlled by relatively small objects, a bridle and a rudder respectively. The tongue, like a bridle or a rudder, can either get you into trouble or keep you free from difficulty depending on how you use it. Though small, it can have tremendous impact. The size of the tongue is not a measure of its importance.

Third, James 3:6 maintains the tongue has the potential for both great and terrible things. The image James uses is fire. Under controlled conditions, like cooking on a stove, it is very useful. Without controlled conditions, like wildfires that consume thousands of acres of trees and wildlife, it is destructive. Leaders must be ever aware that what they say is taken very seriously by those that hear them.

Fourth, James 3:7-8 states the tongue is something that must be trained. Learning to speak is a skill that goes far beyond infancy.

Developing the ability to control your words and speak properly is a life-long process. The Bible tells us that the mouth conveys what the mind and heart conceive. Pay attention to what is in your heart and mind, for it will be evident to others in your speech.

Fifth, James 3:9-12 calls us to remember that both godly and ungodly speech come from the same instrument, the tongue. Even after we accept the Lord Jesus as Savior and receive a new nature, the old, unredeemed nature is still alive and active whenever our guard is let down. While Scripture warns repeatedly about unprofitable words, here it is sharply defined as holy and unholy speech coming from the same mouth. Guarding both our thoughts and words is a full time job.

The Bible emphasizes the serious spiritual consequences of tampering with the truth. The reasons for this are clear: 1) truth aligns us with God, 2) we are redeemed to reflect God's character, and 3) truth-telling is a matter of submission to God's will. Common distortions of the truth include:

- Assuming something to be true when it is false
- Beguilement, the sharing of false information
- Boasting
- Deceit
- Exaggeration
- False witnessing
- Flattery
- Gossip
- Griping
- Lying
- Slander

Years ago it was reported that to train bank employees and other financial experts to recognize counterfeit money, these people would be exposed to stacks of real money so that when counterfeit currency would show up it would be easily recognizable. If you know the real stuff you will be able to quickly spot the phony stuff. I believe this idea holds true for avoiding the pitfall of careless talk. Concentrate on the true, the good and the beautiful and you will quickly recognize that which is not. Surround yourself with friends and colleagues who are committed to truth and integrity. Correct false ideas that are presented to you when you hear them. With the world becoming more and more secular and the rejection of truth becomes more prevalent as time goes by, it is important for Christian leaders to model truth and honesty in every aspect of their personal and business life.

One of the early lessons I learned as a leader was that I could not "think out loud." As a regular employee I was used to normally expressing my opinion on topics whenever I was asked. However, as a leader, even tentative thoughts or possible "solutions" to problems were suddenly taken as final decisions. I had to learn to "put my mind in gear before I put my mouth in motion" or I would find myself creating situations I had not intended to create.

Pause and Reflect

Be quick to listen and slow to speak. Wise leaders have found it very helpful to develop a habit of pausing for a brief time before responding to questions or challenges. It allows you to pray and think before speaking. As I told my four boys when they were growing up, you have two ears and one mouth. Listen twice as long as you speak and then you will have something helpful to say.

The Pitfall of Complacency

One expression that I used to hear fairly regularly from some workers was, "If it ain't broke, don't fix it." The idea apparently was to leave things alone as long as they didn't seem to need any attention. I came to the conclusion that it was a lazy man's view of the world that sprung from the pit of complacency.

What is wrong with a little complacency? Do we have to always be looking for ways to improve things? Can't we leave well enough alone? Simply put, it ignores the concept of continuous improvement and violates a standard of excellence. Instead, complacency refers to past history, makes a subjective comparison with others' performance, or uses the immeasurable standard of personal emotions and feelings. Many organizations today are satisfied to maintain status quo as long they are doing okay. They do not consider what their profit margins could become if they paid more careful attention to improve their business. They are even known for selling products below cost to maintain an image for a very long time. They get trapped in the realm of "okay but not great."

Those who study the future, recognize that paradigm shifts in products and systems of production and delivery are occurring on a near daily basis. Filtering out the right ones from the ones that are not appropriate or profitable is the tough part. Studies have demonstrated that we like to stay with what is tried and true, even if a new pathway appears to be better and potentially more profitable. We hesitate. We often are not open to new thinking or new methods. We hold on to doing what we have done well for many years. In fact, many times the shift in our process, product, or service is not even recognized as a possibility because we are so steeped in our own history and the successes we have achieved up to this point. To begin a new path when the one we are on seems so successful appears to be a very foolish and risky move.

However, if time and change have taught us anything, it is that changes are inevitable and there cannot be any improvement without change. Determining the degree of change, the risks involved, having the right people and safeguards in place, plus having the courage to try new things and invest in the future success of the enterprise is the mark of a wise leader. It is not change for the sake of change, but a designed change with the purpose, goals and values of the business in mind. It is directed and guided change with built in measures of success and control.

One of the ways change is often attempted is in the acquiring of another business or the merger of two similar non-profit organizations. This can be a very good approach if there is an appropriate match of purpose, culture, mission and vision. While this can be an excellent way to overcome stagnancy and complacency, there are things of which to be wary in the process. Whenever one business acquires another business and one is considerably stronger than the other, there is a significant potential for failure. Whenever one business acquires another business that is totally out of their primary industry, product field, or supporting industries, there is significant potential for failure. What works well in one field does not necessarily work well in another. When a non-union company acquires a union company, or vice versa, there is a significant potential for failure. It is not merely a matter of lining up the right legal structures and agreements. The problems lie in the fact that the cultures, mission statements and values of the two types of businesses are not normally harmonious. While there is value to be gained through the experience, the merger or acquisition will normally be short lived and can be very expensive.

An organization does not have to go for dramatic change in order to avoid complacency. Well planned and measured steps on a regular and timed basis will help keep the enterprise fresh and visionary. Put in place senior leadership with diverse and complimentary styles; yet with common values and a solid commitment to the mission and vision of the company. Whenever an organization has been successfully doing the same thing for five or more years, it is the responsibility of the leader to examine the process and results and look for new ways to enrich and improve. Only by a constant process of renewal and continual improvement can a business or organization expect to remain competitive and successful. Not all change is improvement, but you cannot improve without change. Change that is accomplished in the right way with the right motives and process is the leader's goal. Be a change agent and lead with a prayerful heart and a careful mind. Guide the change, don't fight it!

Pause and Reflect

Is your life displaying signs of complacency? What are the symp-toms? Any indications of complacency in your organization?

What change(s) would make the biggest difference in your busi-ness in terms of value and profit to the company? What steps do you need to take to make those changes? Who is the best one in the company to lead such a change?

Pause and reflect on what the future could be for your organization if you were to make these changes and put your group in the posi-tion of being an industry innovator and leader.

The Pitfall of Excuses

If you have recognized the problem of complacency in the preceding section then you will be familiar with the list of excuses that people make to justify their complacency. "We don't have the right staff," "We don't attract enough customers or clients," "We don't have a good location," "We don't have the finances to do the job right," "Our product or service mix isn't right," "The economy is hurting us" and so the excuses multiply. What are the problems? Are these real issues or simply excuses? Someone has defined an excuse as "the skin of a reason, wrapped in a lie." We are fairly proficient at devel-oping excuses but not very productive in answering them. It is often easier to ignore the excuse-makers than deal with their negativity.

Everyone has offered excuses from time to time. It is the easy way to avoid revealing the real problem, or the fastest route out of a difficult situation. All the same, excuses are a form of lying and when exposed, generally create more problems. Lying is very pervasive in our day, but this is nothing new. The first sin in the Garden of Eden was not Eve's partaking of the forbidden fruit, but Satan's lying to Eve about God and the consequences of her proposed action. Lying is at the heart of most sinful situations and cannot be excused on the basis of size or color. There are no small lies and a white lie is still a lie. Excuses are no more than disguised lies.

Favorite situations for excuses include things like missing deadlines, being late for a meeting, not delivering what the customer ordered, failure to follow through on an assignment, being where one is not supposed to be, behavior that is unacceptable in the company, or inappropriate public actions. Excuses in our personal lives often spring from trying to hide more wrongful behavior, covering a bad habit, or a getting out of some situation where honesty would reveal your true heart and mind. Making excuses may be a response mechanism that has been developed and refined over a period of time.

How should a leader respond to an excuse-maker? It is critical to recognize and deal with the excuse (the real sin that is occurring at the moment) and then establish criteria whereby you, as the leader, can properly monitor, correct and if finally necessary, dismiss the offending party.

Leaders have a responsibility to a myriad of entities: the company, owners, investors, productive and cooperative workers, suppliers, clients or customers as well as the general public. And all have the reasonable expectation of truthfulness, to be treated in an open, ingenuous manner and to uphold honesty throughout the enterprise. It is an awesome responsibility that is placed on leaders, yet necessary if the organization is to maintain a positive reputation. Excuses must be recognized for what they are and eliminated if truth and integrity are going to be honored.

Stakeholders expect truth from our organization leaders. They anticipate a certain level of attention to their needs in relation to the main business. Our stakeholders include our investors or owners, ourselves as leaders of the enterprise, our employees, our customers, our vendors, our communities and the official regulatory bodies specific to each industry. It is more than just a matter of delivering a profit for a business, but also delivering truth and value to each stakeholder in the process. A wise leader focuses on what will benefit the stakeholders, but also recognizes that some expectations may be in competition with others.

The best way to address this is to develop a list of values to which the enterprise is committed and coordinate that list with the various stakeholder expectations. This can then become a tool for the leader in determining the level of success that is being achieved by the organization at various stages of development. The expectations of each group are different and need to be acknowledged as special targets to be achieved.

- The **owners** or **investors** expect the leadership to be honest and deliver on the goals and promises that have been established and to formulate a strategic plan for continued growth and improvement.
- The company **leadership** expects to make a profit and meet or exceed the strategic plan goals. They expect to be properly appreciated and rewarded and given the appropriate support by ownership that strengthens the entire organization, with competent employees that are committed to their work.
- The **employees** expect the organization to function according to its stated mission, vision, policies and procedures and meet their personal financial and safety needs by creating productive jobs in a supportive work environment.
- The **customers** and **consumers** expect quality products and services at fair and competitive prices with reliable and appropriate information.
- The **vendors** expect accurate specifications, clear operational policies, reasonable delivery schedules, fair remuneration and prompt payment.
- The **communities** in which the companies operate expect companies to maintain a profitable business, to be ethically and socially responsible and to respect and support worthwhile civic endeavors.
- The **regulators** expect organizations to provide safe, quality products and services, with the highest ethical principles and policies, at a fair price, while meeting the professional and legal standards of the community and industry.

Good leaders desire to go beyond the minimum expectations and strive to be frontrunners in the industry by adding value wherever possible to both products and services. They recognize their business strengths and weaknesses and build upon the strengths while improving the weak areas so the enterprise and its output are never knowingly compromised. Weaknesses are never excused but corrected to insure continued growth and profitability. The company's strategic plan is their roadmap for improvement. Benchmark organizations seek to be the best and set a standard for excellence in their respective fields.

Pause and Reflect

Listen to the ebb and flow of conversations surrounding your organization. What excuses do you hear? Describe any common threads that emerge and develop appropriate solutions for the problem.

What is your group's place in the competitive industry where you exist? What are the things that need improvement or correction in your operation?

What role will you play in bringing your organization to a higher and more profitable level of operation over the next six to twelve months? What individuals or organizations can help you both set and achieve the expectations you desire?

Plan and conduct a high level leadership evaluation and action meeting to involve your impact players (key people) in developing and administering an advancement plan for the company and follow through on the strategy. Set appropriate dates and levels of expectation for various areas of the company performance and begin with those operations and departments that will have the biggest impact on the future success of the enterprise.

The Pitfall of Success

No discussion on the dangers of leadership would be complete without addressing the pitfall of success. In fact, you might be saying to yourself right now, "How in the world can success be a problem?" You work all your life to be a successful leader and it seems that it should be a matter of celebration, not caution. However, it is important for a godly leader to be sensitive to all issues that can make or break them and success is one of those issues.

Success can become a problem if you personally (in your heart and mind, if not in public) begin to take credit for the company's success. It becomes a problem when you do not recognize and give credit to God for all He has done in and through you. It becomes a problem when you do not give the right people the appropriate recognition for the success you enjoy.

For example, some leaders seem to believe that if they give credit to underperformers for a measure of the company's success, these people will step to the plate and become more productive and loyal. Just the opposite happens in most cases. The hard workers begin to resent both the underperformers and the leader who gave them undeserved recognition. After all, employees are not blind to what happens in the organization; most know when recognition is rightfully deserved.

Success can be a problem if the measure of success achieved leads to complacency. The company becomes satisfied with what has been accomplished and does not seek bigger and more valuable growth opportunities. The natural tendency for many people after significant goals have been achieved is to expect "downtime" for rest and relaxation. "You can't keep pushing these people or they will get tired and quit," has been said to many a successful leader by colleagues who want to coast and not overwork themselves. While it is true that schedules and workloads must be balanced to prevent burn out; neither a business nor an individual can rest on past accomplishments and maintain the degree of success for any period of time.

Success can be a problem because it sets you apart from others. Some may consider you a hero to be admired and emulated; others will see you as an enemy to be conquered and eliminated. Being a trend setter, a high achiever, or a benchmark company is an honor but also a threat to the competition. While they might express admiration for your achievement, they are also setting their sights on you for future conquests. The only way to stay in front and lead the field is to continuously search for new and better ways of doing what you do. Both technological and ideological shifts in your industry and related fields will have a huge impact on your future. Be on the lookout for those major changes that can accelerate your business and make it even more successful in the days ahead.

Finally, success can be a problem if it does not result in the improvement of the company morale, productivity, reputation or profitability. These should all, in turn, lead to a stronger, more resilient and satisfied work force and leadership team. If the employees and customers do not see and experience the benefits of success in some tangible way, they will be disappointed and future attempts at significant improvements will be hindered. The old expression that success breeds success has much sound thinking behind it. Handled right, your organization's success can be a launching pad for future growth and prosperity. Be a winner and do not rest on past accomplishments. Look for new realms to conquer and victories to achieve.

Meet with your top leaders and brainstorm new methods, products and services that can increase your sphere of influence and grow the company. Growth is a sign of new life and freshness. Maintain a positive spirit of innovation and productivity to attract the kind of leaders who thrive in this type of atmosphere. Always be on the lookout for impact players who value the rules, commit to the values and share the culture. You will enjoy the benefits of success and avoid the pitfalls that come along with success. Be all that God intends for you to be and always give Him the glory.

Pause and Reflect

Consider any pitfalls of success into which you may have stumbled. From your employees' perspective, are you giving credit where credit is due? Do your company stakeholders appropriately benefit from your success?

What change, however small, would increase you effectiveness and make you more successful?

Who is the single most competitive rival in your industry? What are they doing that makes them so competitive? What can you do to overtake their competitive edge and lead the field?

Who are the key leaders you need to help you with your vision and leadership to strengthen your company? What are you doing to recruit and train these people for success in the days ahead? Do you have a written plan for company improvement and financial success? Gather key leaders in the company and discuss these questions.

CHAPTER 4

PARTICIPATORY LEADERSHIP

WHILE leadership has begun to gain greater appreciation by more and more segments in both the business and non-profit worlds; the particular type of leadership that has gained acceptability has also changed. In the past, single, strong, directional styles of leadership were predominant. The general idea was that if you were in a leadership position you were entitled to do things your way and have things done your way, regardless of the methods used. It was somewhat assumed that you were there by divine right. "Might makes right" and "My way or the highway" were expressions that seemed to fit much of this type of leadership.

As time went on, a more democratic style of leadership became popular. Most leaders no longer demanded compliance but provided incentives and opportunities for followers to contribute their ideas and innovations to the management process and share to some degree in the rewards of success. While it was not exactly an "equal vote" type of system, channels were established for employees to contribute their recommendations and ideas for company advancement and success.

In more recent years the theme has been a type of leadership style identified with the term participatory management or team leadership. While it is often defined and understood in very different ways, it has been generally recognized that the innovative organization accomplishes a high proportion of its productive changes through the active involvement and participation of team members. Involving people at all levels in participative teams with control over their own outcomes helps the organization develop and utilize more and better ideas to improve performance and increase future skills. This is often done in the form of defined structures called task forces, quality circles, problem-solving groups, shared-responsibility teams, or similar names. The terms used to describe this type of leadership change with the passage of time but the central idea remains the same. Valuable people sharing their knowledge, skills and experience with one another, will bring about the most productive outcomes.

Leading Like a Cowboy or a Shepherd?

The images of a cowboy and a shepherd have been used to describe leaders in many books on management and leadership. The first pictures someone sitting high up on a stallion with rope in one hand and a whip in hand, herding the cattle along a dusty trail in spite of what they want to do.

The other portrays an individual with staff in hand, walking in front of the sheep to gently guide them over rough terrain to a peaceful and prepared pasture. The first tends to picture the leader as boss, while the second tries to picture the leader as a partner involved in the process. While neither illustration is complete, each has some truth to convey. The question is how to determine if participatory leadership and participatory management styles are best for your company.

While there are many ways to approach this question, the wise leader will establish a series of criteria to help guide the process of analysis. The criteria include things like the rate of change in the industry, the quality of personnel in the organization, the ability of the employees to positively deal with controversial issues, adaptation to new methods, confronting vested interests in the group and the patience to see new programs and procedures implemented through the initial phases of the change process. Change is an immense concern for leaders. If the company wants to get ahead and stay ahead of the competition, it is important to develop people by having them participate in learning new skills, gathering new information and broadening their viewpoints through new contacts.

Admittedly, situations occasionally arise where participatory management may not be the optimal approach. There may be one person in your group whose expertise in a particular area far exceeds all others. There may be situations when multiple inputs from many individuals will slow and confuse progress. This can occur when the task is already part of someone's regular responsibilities; when most of the team works more productively alone; when no one has any passion for the task; or when the process of working together will neither enrich nor develop the knowledge, skills or abilities of the group. Some people just need to work alone.

Beginning a Participatory Structure

Not everyone will be thrilled by an announcement that the company is changing from a present leadership style to a new one. In fact, the way it is introduced can spell the difference between success and failure. The first mistake leaders often make is to introduce a participatory style by decree. It is something the top manager orders the middle managers to do for the rest of the employees. This imposition of a participatory structure may cause significant opposition. However, there is an ideal middle ground that involves both team managers and employees in making decisions by exposing them to the same information the leader has and by making the leader's thought process transparent.

Just because change is a good idea and may produce a better work environment does not mean that everyone will comfortably buy into the new proposal. If employees perceive that the new style of leadership is being imposed on them from above for their "own good," it will be tough to implement. Leaders can easily fall into a paternalism trap by treating participation as a gift to others rather than something that has been earned; or a luxury, rather than a results-oriented, task-related organizational tool. Being able to fully involve your team in the process of deciding and implementing leadership change will demonstrate the benefits of participatory management better than almost anything else.

Every organization, by definition, needs some type of structure. Erich Fromm's classic book, *Escape from Freedom*, addresses the problems people face when they are given freedoms they cannot handle.[13] Fromm proposed that true freedom is not the absence of structure – letting the employee go off and do whatever they want – but rather a clear structure which enables people to work within established boundaries in an autonomous and creative way. Structure means giving people full information regarding the ground rules and providing them with patterns to help develop their process.

Some leaders fear that delegating responsibilities to others means abdicating responsibility for monitoring and supporting the leadership process. However, the truth is that most people look to leaders to guide and help direct the process. True delegation involves a proper balance of freedom and control. If the one who delegates and the one who receives the delegation will define the process and agree on the end result, it will work smoothly. When there is a breakdown in the understanding and agreement between leader and follower, the delegation process fails. Delegating responsibilities to other people does not mean abdicating responsibility for monitoring and supporting the project. When a leader fails to maintain some type of follow-up contact or reporting system with followers, it can be interpreted as neglect or disinterest rather than confidence. People frequently want their leaders to provide guidance, understand the scope of their efforts and demonstrate appreciation for the work accomplished.

---

13 Eric Fromm, *Escape from Freedom* (New York: Henry Holt and Company, 1994) 320 pp.

The participatory style of decision-making is time consuming, which is a concern for many leaders. Not only will it absorb a bit more of your time, but it will take time away from other employees and their core responsibilities. Time is not an unlimited resource and time spent in one area means less time available somewhere else. The way to balance this is to legitimatize participative activities and entitle participants to take time for them as long as they can still do their core jobs effectively.

Employees feel an obligation to their core tasks, but the more time and energy that participation appears to take away from those functions without a compensating reward, the more it will be resisted. People need to feel that their scant time is well spent on activities that produce tangible and visible results. In assigning tasks for participation, they need to be clear, concrete and likely to produce a solid outcome. For a while, participation is indeed rewarding in and of itself, especially if it is novel and exciting and provides access to higher level management as well as the enjoyment of working in a spirited team. But people also want more than that as time goes on. Settling the issue of credit and recognition is important at the outset of the process or greater problems can be created in the future.

Identifying Inequities

Even in the best of managerial and leadership practices, inequities can arise. For example, teams that are pulled together from different areas, with awareness that they will be returning to their original jobs, may slip into deference patterns. Individuals with higher status are given more airtime, their opinions carry more weight and they generally enjoy a privileged position within the group.

Knowledge and information are needed to contribute effectively to task teams. When there is a knowledge gap that is not closed with information before the team meets, inequalities develop that are often frustrating to the less informed members of the group. They respond by dropping out or failing to appear in meetings. Further, there may be an unequal distribution of skill and personal resources.

People bring to groups different levels of experience, verbal skill, personal qualities, access to information-bearing networks and interest in the task. Specific skills involved in articulating opinions, developing arguments and reaching decisions are differently distributed across the organization. People in certain positions tend to have better developed skill sets for effective participation – the ability to push a point of view, ability to see issues in context and so on.

Finally, outsiders, newcomers, or those not attending meetings regularly often feel uncomfortable about speaking up, especially if the group has developed its own language, abbreviations or understandings.

All of these issues need to be resolved before the participatory leadership-management process can become effective. It is much for a leader to consider when faced with the question of improving the climate, changing the culture and raising the productivity levels of a business operation. When properly addressed, however, it is a winning process well worth the investment.

Pause and Reflect

What leadership style would your team say best describes your organization and why? Are you using participatory groups within your departments? If so, rate their effectiveness. What inequities may exist within the group(s)? How well do your employees balance their participatory involvement against their core responsibilities?

Think through a completed project that you delegated to a group. Were you satisfied with the result? Did you maintain regular contact with the group? How often did they request input or guidance from you? In what way did you express appreciation for their work?

Review the culture and climate of your organization. What are the most significant, distinguishing marks of your business? What key words come to mind when your organization's name is presented? Discover what words others might use to describe your company. Conduct a survey both internally and externally among customers and competitors alike to get a clearer picture of what the public perception of your business strengths and weaknesses are. Compile a list of your findings to review and determine what you want to strengthen in the business in terms of perceptions and what you would like to eliminate.

Building the Team

If you have ever been involved in Little League or a children's athletic program you know that the first time prospective players get together it never resembles a team. It is more like a gathering of interested but competitive kids jockeying for position. Unfortunately, there are groups that never outgrow that stage of development. Declaring people a team does not automatically make them one. In like manner, decisions in which many people have a voice does not guarantee a democracy.

How much the differing needs and interests of various people in the group will politicize it is in large measure a function of how the team is organized. Teams can become polarized into distinct factions when there are prior, unresolved tensions between team members. People bring their histories with them. The more diverse the cultural and organizational backgrounds of team members, the more difficult it is to meld them into a fully cooperative and productive team culture.

A predominant myth surrounding the idea of "team" is that differences between team members disappear once the team is formed. The myth says that differences no longer exist because all the individuals will submit themselves to the team concept. Everyone has to act as if they were all sharing equally in the operation of the group. While inside the team, they have to pretend they do not see that some are more capable than others, or that some are dominating the group, or that the chair is railroading through another decision. Where "team" mythology is strong, only an outsider – a consultant or facilitator – can break through and help the team honestly evaluate its assumptions and actions and view things objectively.

On the other end of the spectrum lurks another type of danger.

Effective working units often develop tight bonds between members. When problems arise, people tend to be fearful of hurting team-mates' feelings or damaging relationships. Sometimes this hampers open communication regarding problems relating to the team project. While there are positive aspects to close team relationships, it is important to train team members to differentiate between personal loyalties, friendships and working responsibilities. This is something that leaders need to keep in mind as they build effective working units.

There are a number of things to consider as you create teams within your organization. One is the problem of personnel turnover. It would be great if you could count on individuals to be involved with the team for a lengthy period of time. Longevity has the advantage of allowing team members to know each other well enough to recognize each other's strengths and weaknesses.

Something that can temporarily diminish the effectiveness of a team is the addition of new people or the absence of team members. Obviously, absent members and newly appointed people need to be brought up to date on prior discussions and decisions. The group must determine the best way to do that and how much past decisions and discussions need to be revisited with input from the new or absent members. Wise leaders have a procedure for smoothly blending the experienced and the newer team members. Time is invested outside of normal meetings to bring absent and new team members up to date. This, if seen as relation building and saving the team extra time in the meetings, can be a very positive factor. It aids the team in moving forward in the pursuit of their goals.

Some teams are hampered, not by a lack of team spirit or cama-raderie, but by excessive familiarity and insufficient professionalism. While team spirit is a positive aspect, the groups can become so self-focused that they begin to close themselves off from the rest of the business. Team spirit is a valuable element of team-building when properly balanced with the rest of the organizational structure and climate. This leads to the larger question of how to best connect an effective team with the rest of the organization. There are times when a team is working on an issue that impacts several other parts of the company. Establish at the outset how affected areas will be brought into the process so that their vested interests are properly represented. This comes under the heading of power; when leaders recognizes that knowledge acquisition and decision-making are two very powerful elements in organizational life, they will be alert to handle them with care.

Some leaders have discovered that when dividing an organization up into work teams, individual units take on an independent spirit and adopt an ownership perspective that can be detrimental to the health of the entire company. It can even get to the point where if the team did not initiate the new idea or launch the new project, then it is not considered a worthwhile activity. They may go so far as to undermine and defeat it even though in the larger picture, it may be the best thing in the world for the company to pursue. Particularly in larger organizations, an emphasis on participatory management appears to suggest that everyone will have a voice in new methods, products, systems, or markets. Reality says that the constraints of time, money, talent and a host of other factors will dictate that it will not be a true democracy with equal votes for all employees on all projects.

A practical truth for leaders is that teams not only need a good birthing process, but there are times when a proper burial is also in order. Some teams (committees or task forces as well) take on a life of their own and continue to function for a long time without being very productive for the business. Involvement by the individuals on the team may be high, but group productivity may have declined. When this happens it is time to reassess the structures, evaluate the participants, redefine goals and make the needed changes. Upsetting the status quo is rarely popular, but often necessary if you are to reinvigorate the business and increase the success of the operation. With all types of groups and teams you need to alternate periods of intense activity with periods of less intense activity in order to give people the energy to continue. The varying levels can be an ideal time to accomplish changes in the structure and have former teams winding down while newer teams are starting up. This is healthy for a business and for the people involved.

Pause and Reflect

In what areas in your organization are teams, or some organizational representation of teamwork most evident? How do you think a culture of teams and teamwork will affect your work overall? As you review the entire operation, what areas might be enhanced by the introduction of teams and a teamwork philosophy? What areas might be negatively affected if this type of change were to be introduced? If you would like to begin to introduce the concept of teams as a working structure, which area would be the best to start with in terms of potential success and a low risk for failure? Discuss among your key impact leaders how this concept can either help or hinder your company growth and profitability.

The Best or Good Enough?

Every leader has probably had the dream of establishing a perfect organization, one that is not only structured properly but operates at peak efficiency. More than one leader has silently said, "I have a dream" as they contemplated their enterprise. However, at some point reality sets in and you realize that it takes a huge amount of work to produce a quality operation and the perfect organization has yet to be formed. If perfect means problem-free, you will never be there. The sin factor in this world has ruled out perfection, but the grace factor has provided a way of successfully living and serving. What you need to strive for in the workplace are quality products, services and processes, created by productive and successful people, who live satisfying and rewarding lives, contribute positively to the people and world around them, while being morally and ethically committed to godly living.

If we are not going to have utopia, what can we expect? *The leader who has a positive attitude and a commitment to excellence will expect continuous improvement to be the focus of the entire team.* It will be something that is talked about throughout the company, highlighted in reports and presentations and properly rewarded in public meetings. This does not mean that every part of the company will be error free or produce at maximum capacity, but it does mean that there will be a striving for excellence in all areas. While there will likely be a variation in quality and productivity from department to department, the general trend will be upward and employee satisfaction will show a marked improvement.

Once team members begin to experience decision-making on a small scale, the likelihood of their desire to have it on a larger scale is greatly increased. It has been documented that when employees have a chance to develop their own work systems or personal programs they generally become more loyal and want to have more involvement in the organization. While this is not guaranteed, studies at major technological companies have indicated that caution must be the rule when instituting participative leadership programs. There are situations that can be best served by any one of a number of leadership styles. No one size fits all, but to help create independent thinking, self-reliant team members, it has been found that the more participative styles of leadership seem to produce better results.

The Need for Balance

Participative types of leadership and management styles appear to be more effective when you have a well developed management process. A favorable setting for the participative management style includes a clearly designed organizational structure, the appropriate assignment of people to skilled positions, clear assignments and job descriptions that detail manageable tasks, a tested training program, a method to insure broad participation and a proper reward system.

Seek well qualified people, interview them properly and then hire the right ones. This is a critical element to your success. Field

Marshall Montgomery, the famed general of the British Army in World War II, said that leadership success could be traced to the ability to find the right person for the job and then let them do it. A search and hiring procedure is discussed in another section of this book but it is important to state here that leaders bear a huge responsibility for success or failure in this area. The leader must know the job that needs to be done and interview carefully to ascertain objective evidence of an applicant's experience and preparation. The leader must then identify the skills, knowledge, personal qualities and past performance in some related field or position in order to best predict success in the job under consideration. When leaders hire employees because they similarities to their own qualities or personality, they will normally live to regret their choice. The same is true when they hire someone because they are closest at hand and immediately available.

It is expensive to hire the wrong person, considering the time and money invested in the search and selection process, formal training and on the job training time and costs. In addition, the loss of productivity in the early stages of work can mount up to a tidy sum in almost every industry. It is most important to place people in positions where they have a high degree of potential success. Too often this critical task is assigned to an office like Human Resources where they are supposed to select people for widely differing positions. While HR is helpful for many of the legal and detailed aspect of hiring, there is no substitute for the immediate supervisor being well trained and fully involved in the hiring process for the people in their areas. When this is neglected there is generally a loss of quality and productivity and an increase in cost due to the poor alignment of talent and work.

Pause and Reflect

What are your current standards for worker productivity? When seeking new team members, what are the key characteristics and experience basis that you seek? Who is ultimately responsible for *the search and hiring process? Gather your key leaders together and discuss what you need in the workforce to enrich the company talent pool and increase overall productivity. Then make some initial decisions on how to reach the levels of productivity and profit you seek. **People are your most important asset and attention to their welfare, enrichment of talents, skills and vision for the future, is vital to the future growth and development of the business.***

A Posse, a Group or a Team?

Just because there is a gathering of people in a defined space does not mean you have a group or a team. In the old west, they would round up a band of men and set out on the trail of some renegade outlaws with little to no training, experience, order or design. The objective seemed simple, the passion was there, but more problems were created than solved if the reports of those days are to be believed. The posse approach often led to the wrong men being caught, pursuers being killed through carelessness and the criminals getting away with their crimes. The posse approach is not a good model for today's business world.

What about the group approach? A group is a collection of people centered on a common interest with vaguely defined purposes. Characteristically, people in a group generally work independently and sometimes come into conflict because of very different values and purposes. They are much more likely to do what they are told rather than be asked for help in defining the tasks and suggestions for project improvements. Those who are group members versus team members may distrust others in the group because the roles of the various members are not generally defined or coordinated. Additionally, participation in making decisions that impacts the group may be limited. While group members can have ample preparation and training for the job, most group leaders tend to limit the involvement of the group members and control the situation more directly.

On the other hand team members, while differing widely in their talents, experiences, roles and positions, generally have a sense of ownership for their jobs and are much more likely to be committed to goals when they have helped establish them. They are more likely to recognize their responsibility to understand and support the team goals and work toward the success of the team. Unique abilities and contributions are more readily identified and a climate of trust is more prevalent. In addition, a wider range of participation, including the expression of opinions, disagreements, ideas and feelings are encouraged. While team members realize that the leader must be accountable and responsible for the final decisions, they understand their contributions of facts, opinions, and evaluative comments are a valuable part of the dynamic and progressive process. A team is much more likely to take on an identifiable team style and personality as they work toward a common goal, than would a group under the same circumstances.

Leadership Differences

One of the most significant differences between groups and teams can be found in the manner of leaders. A group tends to be led by people who are more management oriented whereas teams tend to be led by people who are more leadership oriented. While in the total scheme of things both managers and leaders are needed, the two styles do produce different results. Let's examine a few of the differences.

Group focused managers are generally very committed to achieving the goals that have been established. They may have warm and friendly personalities but because of the pressure for productivity and the competitive nature of their industry, they may tend to control the flow of information and be more defensive when answering inquiries they deem intrusive or even inappropriate. While they will involve people in some aspects of planning and decision making, they always are careful to limit the scope of others' involvement. In fact, some may even consider group problem-solving activities a waste of time. Group managers who find themselves in circumstances where conflict is present, are uncomfortable with such tension and as a result are slower to respond with solutions. Some will even take on extra subordinates as direct reports to help eliminate personality conflicts between some of their subordinates, rather than work on resolving the conflict directly. When it comes to rewards, they are slow to recognize the achievements of others.

Team centered managers are generally more adept at identifying and managing the potentials and talents in people than they are at achieving defined goals. While not ignoring the immediate goals, they tend to be more visionary and as a result focus on long range goals. The team leader has a passion for getting people involved and committed to the long range picture and tends to seek people who desire to be impact players; those committed to working with like-minded individuals while encouraging others and helping facilitate a winning attitude. They identify conflict situations that may be surfacing and seek to resolve them before they become destructive. They make commitments and keep them. They practice open communication and encourage the asking of questions. However, they may intimidate other leaders whose style is different from theirs. If there is any element of jealousy present in the organization, it can stir up problems for others who may be insecure, inept, insincere, unethical, and/or insubordinate. Team leaders walk a fine line between being strong and misunderstood at the same time.

Trust is an essential part of the team building experience. Trust has been defined as reliance on another's integrity, veracity and faith, so that you would follow that person without fear or misgivings. The person has demonstrated a pattern of behavior that engenders confidence and one worthy of your full commitment. When this is entered into the equation of leadership, it is important to ask yourself about the trust level in your company or organization. What is the level of trust among the leadership, as well as between the leadership and the rest of the employees? Honesty is becoming a rarity in many segments of our world these days. When you find a company that exhibits honesty in their internal and external actions, as well as in their official and unofficial declarations, you have found a worthy company. Emulate it, join it and praise it, for it is becoming an increasingly rare breed.

There are many forms of recognition but the most important is praise. Praise needs to be given when earned and rewards the giver as well as the receiver. Praise needs to be honest, proportionate to the work performed and consistently applied. Become a leader who majors in praise.

Pause and Reflect

With the help of an outside consultant, review the personnel in your company. Department by department, identify the cultural ethos that has developed in each area and determine whether or not what exists is in the best interest of the company. Pick the department that is both the easiest to change and that will have an impact on both the bottom line and the overall company culture. Start your educational process there. Give each department time to adjust and become comfortable with the change before moving on to other areas of the organization. Take a long range view as you seek to build a harmonious and consistent team oriented workforce. The end result will be worth the effort.

The Art of Asking Questions

The ability to ask perceptive questions both in gathering information and evaluating information sets a professionally skilled leader apart from others. Questions open the way for understanding and are effective tools for learning. In ancient times a person was considered wise if they could ask insightful and penetrating questions. When Jesus was a young lad, his parents realized he was missing on the journey from Jerusalem back to Nazareth. They found him remaining in Jerusalem, deep in discussion with the leading scholars of his day. The Bible records that the scholars were surprised to find a young man of his age with such great wisdom. The reference is made primarily to the questions he asked rather than the answers he gave. To ask searching, quality questions, one must have a firm grasp of the subject matter at hand.

On a more personal note, recall your last visit to a physician. What happened when you walked into the examination room? The doctor asked questions. You were the information source. A series of questions were asked to fit a format, a system of information gathering that the doctor needed in order to properly diagnose and treat you. The same holds for other professions. A skillful attorney has learned the art of asking questions in order to better understand the legal issues involved in the problems he has to address.

A manager gets results through other people. It is obvious that the higher a person is in the organization, the greater the distance there is from the "grassroots." Being disconnected from the realities of the daily routines and issues, leaders can get to the place where they do not know enough about all the matters they are called upon to plan, resolve, or advance. In order to be the kind of leader that will make a positive difference in the workplace and understand what your employees know firsthand by experience, learn to ask insightful questions, the right questions, in the correct order. This will help you be well informed and have the proper information to afford wise counsel.

Learning to ask the right questions, at the right time, in the right place, with the right degree of inquiry is an art to be learned. What is important to realize is that the formulation of good questions requires an understanding of the nature of your business. A good question fits into what is referred to as the middle process of thinking. This is the structuring of your thoughts so that you are internally seeking answers to the faithful friends known as "who, what, where, when, why, how and so what." There is a systematic and clear-cut path of ordered questions that can lead to greater and deeper information. Also, a good question can withstand the query, "Why do you ask?" A good question has purpose; it fits into the process and is neither general nor undefined. It asks for specific kinds of information while at the same time allowing the information source to provide other needed data. A good question can build people up and grants them dignity. It recognizes and appreciates the contribution that the person can make to the situation under consideration. It allows individuals to share their mind and heart and gives the effective leader an insight into the individual's life, values and competencies. The individual will also know that the leader is willing to listen to what they have to say.

Good questions seek to allow the respondent to share more than brief facts, as a good question asks for comparisons and distinctions versus similarities. It seeks in-depth analysis and personal perspective. In short, a good question forces a person to think. An open-ended question is generally more helpful than a closed-ended question. The open-ended question normally takes an essay type format while the closed-ended question elicits more of a true/false or yes/no type of response. The open-ended question asks for opinions, experience, desires, facts, comparisons and other data in various combinations. The closed-ended question tends to shut down communication because it appears to render a judgment rather than provide information to assist in the decision process.

This is not to say that closed-ended questions are always improper. While open-ended essay questions may be preferable, they should not be used exclusively. One can go overboard in the direction of explanation versus direct and brief answers. There is a place for factual, closed-ended questions. Another danger is to become too open-ended or too general, so that the person responding takes off in a different direction than the one you intended.

Finally, anticipate periods of silence. Silent periods give individuals a chance to think. Too often a leader, in the drive to be efficient with time, seems to rush discussions and Q & A times. In so doing, they can miss out on significant information and insights.

An exercise that can be very helpful is taking some samples of closed-ended questions and making them more open-ended. Try rewriting the following questions so they encourage greater two-way communication. You can modify the questions to make them fit more closely the work setting that is most familiar to you. Some of these are "leading" questions while others could be viewed as "combative" in nature. Rephrase each one by starting each question with either the words "how" or "what."

1. Is it fair to say that the cost of this new system is too high?
2. Isn't it true that cost cutting is the number one priority here?
3. Why won't this approach work?
4. Do you honestly think that we should not charge for this?
5. Why didn't you tell me that we could not do this in the time allotted?

Make a list of the type of questions you face on a daily basis. Which ones are designed for you to respond with brief, closed-ended answers? Which ones are the kind that you can respond to with ease and appropriate helpful information? Practice the art of asking questions. Let the famous friends of inquiry be your constant companions when it comes to dialoging with colleagues and subordinates alike. The art of asking questions is the mark of an insightful and intelligent leader. I have always been impressed by the fact that when situations became combative or tense, Jesus was known for asking questions rather than just providing answers, even though there was never a person on earth who had all the right answers as did He.

Pause and Reflect

What is your leadership style? If you are not certain what your style is get one or more of the current style analysis worksheets and test yourself. Knowing what your leadership style is and what the styles of your colleagues are can go a long way toward helping you lead and manage successfully. Balance is a significant part of being a successful leader. For example, if you are naturally gifted as one who is comfortable and effective in leadership that seeks to draw people out through the use of open ended questions and discussion, maximize your gift as you lead but do not avoid answering questions posed by employees. On the other hand, if you are more of a directive and expressive leader and good at presenting ideas and selling them to others, do not try to dramatically change your style but work at seeking the thoughts and ideas of others. Above all, surround yourself with colleagues that have strengths in the areas of your weaknesses. In this way the entire enterprise will be enriched.

Mentoring and Team Building

One of the important opportunities given to a leader is that of influencing and preparing a subordinate who demonstrates potential leadership and discovering ways to further that development. Too many senior leaders have confessed that while they enjoyed leadership, they never took the opportunity to educate and train others to follow in their steps. Today we often use the term "mentoring" to describe the process that was once called developing disciples or developing apprentices. The word mentor comes from the story of a fictional character named Mentor in Homer's mythical story, *Odyssey*. When Odysseus, king of Ithaca, went to fight in the Trojan War, he entrusted the care of his household to Mentor, who served as a teacher and an overseer for Odysseus' son, Telemachus.

After a long and exhausting war, Odysseus was condemned to wander for ten years as he tried in vain to return to his home and family. During his absence from the country, there were some attempts to overthrow him and usurp his throne. In time, Telemachus, now grown to manhood under Mentor's guidance, went in search of his father. According to the myth, Telemachus was accompanied in his search by Athena, goddess of war and the patroness of the arts and industry. Athena assumed the form of Mentor as she guided and instructed him along the way.

Eventually father and son were reunited and together they defeated the would-be usurpers of Odysseus' throne and Telemachus' birthright. In time the word "mentor" became synonymous with a trusted advisor, friend, teacher and wise person. One of the best ways to extend your leadership influence into the future is to invest yourself in the development and training of others who can catch your vision, learn your skills and techniques, understand your values and reproduce future leaders with similar passions and abilities.

It is important to realize that mentors are helpers. Their styles may range from that of a persistent encourager, who helps to build self-confidence to that of a strict taskmaster who teaches us to appreciate excellence and performance. Whatever the style and whatever the approach, these are people who care for others and are seeking to encourage and develop individuals to improve themselves. Mentoring, as a developmental art, was going on long before the Greek classics gave it a name. In fact, it is probably one of the oldest forms of human development. Mentor's job was not merely to raise Telemachus, but to develop him for the responsibilities he was to assume in his lifetime. Mentors still pursue similar tasks.

Mentoring is also one of the broadest methods of encouraging human growth. Today we usually relate mentoring to careers or collegial encouragement, but mentors can touch every facet of a person's being. Let's look at mentoring from a practical viewpoint. Review the following commonly-asked questions regarding important changes in life and reflect on their meaning. As you answer them, do not focus on external events. Rather, concentrate on the developments or changes that occurred within you – the way you saw yourself or others and how your perspective on events may have changed.

1. Who provided an "aha!" experience which allowed you to pierce the core of meaning of some event, in someone, in something, or in yourself? What occurred within you as a result?
2. Who provided you with a quote, or a piece of writing, that had great meaning for you and influenced your thinking or behavior? What is this quote, which you may often repeat and what is its source?

3. Who helped you uncover an aspect, ability, or talent within that had lain dormant until that moment? Describe such an incident. How has this ability or talent helped you in your leadership development and pursuit of excellence?

In the past, most people thought of mentoring as a formal process whereby an older, more mature individual guided a younger person in learning the ropes of an organization or helped further a career move. The term mentoring has been also used to describe the activities of a senior person in the preparation of a junior for a particular office or job and encouraging high standards of performance. In the sponsorship role that senior leaders took in organizations, the term protégé was generally used. In today's globally competitive organizations, many people dislike the word protégé and prefer more neutral terms like mentee, trainee or associate.

Pause and Reflect

It is important to do what you are good at doing. While mentoring is not for everyone, many neglect to even attempt it because they have never seen it done, have never had it done to them, or do not realize how it might be of tremendous importance to others. Building your value system, creative energies and sharing your experiences with others is a tremendous gift to those with lesser experience and knowledge. The more of yourself you give away, the more you gain. Enriching others enriches you in return.

Is Mentoring for You?

As you consider the mentoring possibilities you have in your present working situation, think of three people who have influenced you in some way. Review in some detail what they have contributed to your life in the following areas:

1. Identify someone who inspired you to change the direction of your life in a more positive and constructive way.

2. Think of someone who provided something to help you grow and mature in areas such as depth of feeling, character, or moral and ethical integrity. It could also be someone who has helped you develop a deeper commitment to your values.

3. Name someone who has provided you some form of help at just the right time in your life.

What did these people have in common as coaches or mentors? What were the most evident characteristics they displayed in their life and in their work? Which of their characteristics do you presently have and demonstrate in your leadership work? Being a mentor is not a task to be entered into lightly. It is an awesome opportunity but also a significant responsibility. It is not "making someone else to be like you," but rather helping someone else develop and grow into the type of person who shares your values, appreciates your vision and uses the skills and abilities that God has given them to advance the causes you both share.

At this point you might be asking yourself, "Is mentoring for me?" Mentoring can range from a spur-of-the-moment opportunity to help someone in a unique situation; to an intervention in a critical situation; to an intense, long term relationship. It can take many forms and varying levels of time commitment. Every leader needs to assess where they are at the moment and recognize the conditions that exist before making any serious commitments to mentor someone. A leader's personal interests and work load must also be reappraised from time to time so as to not overload the leader. Sometimes the pursuit of a good goal can keep the leader from pursuing a great goal so discernment is critical.

Consider the following variety of situations:

1. The mentor's resources and the needs of the one being mentored are low, spontaneous, or occasional. Very short-term help may be adequate and satisfying to both parties. Being called upon from time to time for counsel, advice, or specific professional help is desired and sufficient for the individual.

2. The one being mentored often has high demands on the mentor's time, skills and resources. Helping this person find someone else who can be of more help may be appropriate through referral to someone else in the network.

3. The mentor's resources are substantial, but the mentee may have few needs. Occasional help may be all that is required. This would give the mentor time to devote to helping others. One mentor might have several people that they are helping without experiencing overload in such situations.

4. The needs of the one being mentored are high and the mentor's resources are abundant. In such a case this would provide the opportunity for a more intense and productive long term relationship.

Being a Leader Who Mentors

A mentor is a leader and a leader is a learner. Some of the best mentors are people who assume that they, as well as those they mentor, are in a lifelong learning process. In the past it appeared that a person could develop a certain level of wisdom and sophistication and pass along what he or she had learned to those younger and less experienced. In fact, it was expected. In today's world of fast-paced change, this no longer seems to be an option. Leaders today have a difficult time staying on top of the knowledge and skills they need for survival, much less advancing the company. To stay current and productive, keep these thoughts in mind:

1. *Stay focused on basic values, principles and fundamental truths.* This is not a static activity. This is the continual application of fundamental truths to new challenges that require constant reassessment, discussion and even argument from which new wisdom is forged. Every day, justices in the court system, clergy and leaders in industry go through this process of continuous learning.

2. *Keep abreast of new developments and their implications.* This is a more dynamic source of mentoring. It recognizes

that the task of the mentor is self-development; and as such learning and mastery of new concepts is never finished. This is not an unreasonable task if we choose special areas to focus on such as studying the mission of the organization or the latest technology of a specific field.

3. *Mentoring itself is a changing and growing field.*
   If as a mentor, you choose to master active listening, coaching skills, effective confrontation techniques, or new methods of resolving conflict, you are starting on a journey of self-development.

Pause and Reflect

Remember that there is not a single way or form to follow in mentoring. Decide what works for you and try it. By teaching others you enrich yourself, you grow and you contribute to the generations that will come behind you.

Mentoring and Change

Mentoring can be a one-on-one process or even a one-on-small group process. Typically, if it is to succeed it not only has to be endorsed and supported from the top, it needs to be started at the top! It should be recognized that it requires an investment of time and money and clear goals should be established for it to work effectively.

Implicit in the process of mentoring is change. In fact, every type of mentoring situation will involve some type of change. When a mentee is undergoing significant change, he or she usually needs at least five things to be able to adapt successfully. These include: 1) a vision of how their circumstances will look when they have successfully changed; 2) time to absorb the new vision; 3) time to adjust their behaviors and coping mechanisms to manage the stress of change; 4) time to ponder the meaning of change, and finally; 5) time to internalize and own what change is involved. While it is relatively easy to list these requirements, it takes time to assemble the adjustments.

Context shifting can be the key to this process. If a person can clearly imagine what he or she and their world will be like after they have successfully accomplished the desired change, they will do the right things to help them move toward their envisioned goals. This mental adjustment needs to be imagined in positive terms. Too often change is perceived as negative and we create dreaded scenarios rather than positive ones. Helping those being mentored shift mental contexts from today's problems to tomorrow's successes can be exceedingly productive.

There are a number of components in the growth process: helping a person shift his or her mental context, listening when the mentee has a problem, identifying mentee feelings and verifying them through a feedback process, effectively confronting negative intentions or behaviors, providing appropriate information when needed, delegating authority or giving permission for them to move ahead, and finally, encouraging exploration of a variety of options. These seven items are critical components to developing in a healthy and productive manner. The strength lies not in any notion that they meet all the needs of a mentee, but rather they meet major needs. When offered at important junctures in a person's life, they can help that person resolve a problem, make a decision and move ahead.

Productive Confrontation

Very few people are comfortable with and good at confrontation. However, every leader eventually discovers that confrontation is inevitable if one is to maintain the mission and integrity of their organization. When it comes to the mentoring process, sometimes a mentor finds it necessary to confront an attitude, behavior, or some plan that the mentee has developed. However, to criticize, threaten, or pressure the mentee to adopt another course may lower the mentee's self-esteem and may possibly be ineffective in actual accomplishment.

One way to reduce the negative impact of the confrontation process is to adopt what is called "I" messages. This begins with a neutral description of what you, as the mentor, perceive the mentee's message or plan to be. This is followed by a statement of the possible negative effects on both the mentee and other people who might be involved. Finally, you ask the mentee to describe the emotions the intended plan causes within them. The idea is not to tell the mentee how to behave; but rather help them hear, possibly see, but always experience the potential results of their intended course of action. It is designed to have the mentee think through the process in a non-threatening context.

For example, someone you are mentoring has stated that they are going to tell off someone else in another part of the organization. Their statement is something like, "I'm really going to let him have it." The following is a dialogue of *"I"* messages that can be used.

Mentor: "I'm concerned that you are going to give Joe the blast and that such an encounter could badly damage your relationship with his part of the organization."

Mentee: "I don't care, he's got it coming."

Mentor: "Now I'm concerned that you want to go ahead without regard to the consequences."

The basic idea is to have the mentee begin to reflect on what the results of their behavior could be if they follow through with their action plan. In general, mentors want good things to happen to their mentees. They want them to be effective, productive, achieving, successful and happy. However, in their eagerness to help others they may revert to behaviors that prove to be less than helpful. Leadership behaviors that are necessary and important in some situations are not necessarily appropriate in all situations, such as criticizing, giving advice or "rescuing people from their own folly." People can only learn some things only through actual experience. The mentor is not a parent trying to keep their child from all harm. The mentor is more like a teacher who realizes that growth sometimes requires situations where the student can only learn through working out the difficulties alone.

Mentors should be aware that they must keep criticism to a minimum. This does not mean that criticism is eliminated entirely but because criticism is evaluative and judgmental there may be a need to soft peddle it. When we offer "constructive" criticism, we want our message to be helpful. Criticism damages self esteem, generates defensive blocking and drains the energy needed for constructive action. This is a delicate operation because the two most powerful human motivators are survival and security. These motivators are threatened by criticism and evaluation. For some people, criticizing, complaining and nagging are old, self-defeating habits which tend to prolong the problem.

Being aware of the negative aspects of criticism and attempting to avoid criticism does not mean accepting negative behaviors, performance failures, or self-defeating repetitive actions. When a mentee's behavior is not up to snuff, we need to think through what would be an effective intervention. One of the best ways of doing this is to help the mentee think through healthy alternatives to the actions and behaviors they are performing. This is another place where *"I"* messages are very helpful.

Pause and Reflect

Change is never easy but is a continual process. My favorite saying when referring to change is that "I like change – whenever I initiate it." The key to most change situations is to take them in small, incremental steps. For most people, large dramatic changes are difficult to welcome and embrace. If we can help people discover ways to introduce or face change a little at a time, it makes the experience more palatable. Small steps may take longer but are often the safer road to travel.

Mentoring versus Advice-Giving

Many mentors believe that a large part of their job is to give advice to their mentees. However, there is a down-side to providing advice.

When we give advice, we assume we have superior knowledge, insight, or wisdom related to the problem. This may be true in certain situations, but certainly not all of them. If we are engaged in a professional discourse in an area where we have expert knowledge, it might be appropriate to furnish advice. However, when we are dealing with a mentee's personal problem, our mentee is likely to know more about the problem than we ever will. They are living it. When we attempt to give advice or offer suggestions about personal problems, we often encounter frustrating resistance and responses like, *"Yes, but...."*

There are several ways we can serve our mentees in a more effective manner. Listen attentively as they describe their problem. Honestly and carefully feed back the emotions we hear them expressing, to confirm that we not only hear them but understand the deeper, emotional nature of the difficulty. When asked, provide ideas or information, which they can use to weave and develop their own solution.

Those leaders who are effective mentors make a commitment to help others. They share, they model, they counsel, they teach, but they do not take over problems unless there is a crises that requires immediate action. This is generally known as rescuing. In certain situations rescuing is necessary but most mentoring circumstances do not require this action. The world is full of genuine victims, people who through no fault of their own come upon hard times. Often these people need help as when a hurricane strikes, an auto accident occurs, or a business fails and the person loses their job.

Another type of person who needs help is the one who repeats destructive behavior patterns due to feelings of inadequacy, prior victimization, or poor adaptation to some crisis in life. When dysfunctional patterns of behavior occur, a mentor can help by pointing out the repetitive nature of the experience and can possibly use counseling skills to help the mentee realize their situation and begin to break the pattern.

It is important to realize that rescuing the mentee, or attempting to take over the problem, is not likely to provide long term assistance. Temporary help in a crisis may be appropriate, but when there is a recurring pattern of this form of help, the mentor actually becomes a part of the mentee's problem.

In the past, while men mentoring women has been rare, it is becoming more accepted and prevalent. A number of research studies have revealed that there are problems related to cross-gender mentoring based on gossip, envy, suspicion, speculation, false assumptions, sexual stereotypes and charges of sexual harassment. It must be recognized that such attitudes and behavior have lessened the effectiveness of cross-gender mentoring in some environments. Consequently, it is a concern that needs close monitoring.

Of course, as in all potentially difficult situations, there are positive as well as negative potentials. Cross-gender mentoring can enrich the lives of mentees and provide valuable insights and experiences if carried out carefully. A gender-balanced and fairly treated organizational work force is likely to remain more a challenge than a reality for some time. While the objective is a worthy one, the road to success can be rocky.

Another component in mentoring is the issue of cross-cultural communication. The workforce of today has changed significantly in most parts of the country due to ethnic and social diversity. Signs of cultural diversity are virtually everywhere. This diversity represents some of most subtle and special relationships imaginable. Even in relatively homogeneous groupings, differences in economic class, religious background, regional alliances and even family traditions, can create cultural distinctions which then complicate the mentoring task.

Most countries today are discovering that the variety of cultural differences, and our personal responses to them, is a large part of what makes us unique. Our cultural distinction may also enable each of us to appreciate special facets of a problem, as we approach a solution from different angles and contribute to a more comprehensive, elegant and lasting solution. For the mentor this means carefully listening, respecting the variety of differences between individuals and treating all people with respect and dignity. In this manner we can build a stronger, more successful company and make a contribution to our communities and society in general. It is a Herculean task but a goal worth of pursuit.

Pause and Reflect

Mentoring is not for everyone! There are those who are excellent teachers who will never become good mentors. There are leaders who are good role models and managers who are just not equipped to be mentors. Personality, experience, background and training (or lack of it), all seem to be factors. However, it is an opportunity to make a difference in someone else's life that can be very significant on their path to leadership and successful living. It can be a highly organized process or a casual and loosely structured one. Each leader should explore the potentials and pursue the possibilities. It just might be the most important contribution you can make to your business or organization.

CHAPTER 5

How to Hire the Best Employees

ONE of the most critical yet often most dreaded tasks of leadership is searching for and hiring employees. It is exciting to be growing as an organization but to find the right team members is often complicated and difficult. Many a leader is plagued by the time required, the costs involved, the lack of precision and the uncertainty of hiring that after all is said and done, the wrong person may have been employed.

This chapter is designed to lessen the anxiety by providing a systematic and tested approach that will provide the leader with the insights and information regarding candidates that can spell the difference between hiring success and hiring failure. When this process is implemented and your homework is completed, you will make far better decisions and more accurate assessments about applicants. It is all based on the premise that past successful experience in tasks and responsibilities is the best predictor of future success in similar roles.

A Valid Hiring Practice

Finding the right person for the right job is one of the most significant things a leader can do. The late British Field Marshall Montgomery wisely observed: "The essence of leadership is recruiting other leaders. When you do that well, you succeed. When you do that poorly, you fail."

The most commonly used technique for securing the right person is conducting an interview. It is supposed to give you the information you need to evaluate whether a candidate is right for a particular position. There have been interviews as long as one person has required the services of another. While the jobs and applicants may vary, the approach is basically the same: "Let's call them in, look them over, size them up and choose the best one." The candidates offer themselves for examination; the leader in charge ponders and ultimately passes judgment. The conclusion is "I like that one" or "I don't like that one."

If you happen to ask the leader why he prefers one candidate over another, his response may be: "Looks like a winner – good track record." Or he may point to test results, tap his temple and whisper, "Smart!" Most leaders have a hard time explaining why they feel one person will do a better job than another. They can only say that their instincts tell them so. In many cases, the instincts or gut feelings of a seasoned and experienced leader prove correct and his choice for the position does well. Just as often, however, the individual who seemed to be a sure bet for success turns out to be a poor choice.

One of the ways of attempting to ensure a better fit between the candidate and the position is to pay closer attention to the interview process. The skill of the interviewer can make a significant difference in personnel selection. A poor interviewer may not actually listen to the person being interviewed. Many interviewers tend to dominate conversations with their own experience, bits of history, advice or prolonged comments. The assumption appears to be that if the candidate is a good listener, they will be a good worker. Sometimes the interviewer looks for some kind of commonality with the interviewee, such as a shared enthusiasm for basketball. Common interests will strengthen the bonds of friendship but may not be the best indicator of good job performance.

The untrained interviewer often signals the desired response unintentionally by the questions they ask. For instance, if asked, "Did you win any awards in college?" the candidate knows that awards are considered important and may remember the dorm chess tournament or his fraternity's good citizenship award. Candidates typically do not invent past careers but will slant the presentation of themselves to embellish the areas where the interviewer shows the greatest interest. An alert candidate can find accomplishments that play to the interviewer's interests although they may occupy little of his own time or personal devotion. With a speck of encouragement from an interviewer, the candidate will turn a part-time hobby into the central theme of his life. A trained interviewer will ask, "Tell me more about your college activities," instead of "Did you win any awards?" The trained behavior-based interviewer asks general questions designed to unmask the candidate's true concerns instead of leading the applicant to specific details.

Some untrained interviewers are also too easily satisfied with surface facts and do not discover the reasons behind them. The interviewer may find that the applicant did poorly in his senior year but neglect the fact that he was working full-time to earn tuition. If another person did particularly well, was it because he really buckled down or because he skated through an easy course load? Sometimes an interviewer is dramatically impressed by the paper presentation of the candidate because a resume has been carefully developed and packed with information designed to impress although not necessarily related to the job at hand.

Components of Job Potential

A number of factors determine how an individual functions while on the job. Intelligence, experience, motivation and personality combine to make up that person's profile. A good interview separates and measures each of these components, furnishing a more accurate picture of how an individual will perform in a particular role. We will now examine each of these components individually to see how they relate to potential employment success.

Intelligence

Intelligence is extremely difficult to measure. Although intelligence tests can be used as part of the screening process, the results should not be taken as absolute. Different tests measure different skills and scores from one type of test cannot necessarily be equated with scores from another type of test. School records can also be deceptive. College requirements vary and so does the degree of difficulty within different courses. A bright student may dislike his major and not apply himself whereas a mediocre student may grind out a terrific performance. Wise interviewers tend to consider test results and school records but not place excessive weight on them in the final decision. The best way to measure intelligence is to listen to the candidate talk. Does the person provide articulate answers to abstract concepts? Do they offer complete and well considered responses to questions? Do they probe the interviewer for key issues concerning the job and the organization?

Personality

Personality is more than just a distinction between introvert and extrovert. It encompasses the ways in which people handle pressure, balance responsibilities and relate to others. When you examine personality, you are not concerned as much with the candidate's ability to do the job, as with the suitability of their temperament to the job. A candidate's personality must also mesh well with potential colleagues. It is critical to seek out individuals whose personalities will fit well with current colleagues and within the culture of that department and organization at large.

Experience

Experience is another very important factor in the job interview process. The interview techniques that will be suggested in this chapter are heavily based on prior experience and prior skill development. Experience is proven ability that should be directly applicable to the job under consideration; it is an asset ready to work for you *now*. It will be beneficial to your company only to the extent that the individual's experience is the same experience needed in this position. Well before any interviewing process is begun, start by developing a job description and a profile of the employee you are seeking. Resumes offer a few clues, but well-designed questions drawn from a well-designed job description will yield the best results.

Motivation

Motivation, or what coaches call the drive to win, translates to how hard the applicant will try once they are on the job. It is a major indicator of future performance. Skills can be taught, knowledge can be acquired, but motivation cannot be easily developed because it comes from inside. School or work records can tell you a little about a candidate's motivation by showing performance patterns. Careful questioning, however, is the only way to discover why the individual performed as they did. Motivation is concerned not only with the level of drive that exists, but also the reasons why the work they did was accomplished the way it was. People are motivated from a variety of motives. Sometimes it may be money, title, increased responsibility, creative atmosphere, job security, or a variety of other perks that often surround a position. These have to be viewed in the light of each candidate's priority system. For example, an individual who highly values family life will be unhappy traveling away from home most of the week.

Once you decide to examine how each individual functions, everything else about the interview will change. Instead of digging for the facts you need, you allow the individuals to present themselves in their own way. By directing discussion without dominating, you can gear the interview to help the person open up and relax. Everything you do in the interviewing process should coax the candidate to reveal as much as he can about himself as it relates to the position. The better the match, the better off you both will be.

Cultural/Technical/Personality Fit

Often neglected in the hiring process is the fit of the person to the uniqueness of the organization. Every organization, except for those that are in the initial phase of their creation, has an historical, cultural background that shapes its operation. In today's world technology and personality are essential ingredients to be considered as well. With the explosion of technology younger generations have become so immersed and comfortable with the technology that it is expected that it will dominate their performance.

When I need some adjustment to my television or other electronics, I rely on my sons or grandsons to fix the problem for me. Even for the chart preparation for this manuscript I sought help from a high school young man, for who things like this are simple and easy. For me, anything on the computer beyond word processing and e-mail is a mystery. Further than that, I seek the help of a younger individual who enjoys and understands the technological tools. In our organizations today, cultural, technological and personality assessment must be part of our hiring toolbox if we want to secure the right team players.

Pause and Reflect

Of your current employees, who are the best workers? Where did they come from? What attitudes, skills and knowledge do they possess that make them superior team members? What types of things are you doing in recruiting, interviewing and training new employees that will insure a continuous flow of good workers and leaders? Review all your current hiring practices to make certain that you are getting the best prospects.

The Interview Process

Designing the interview process is extremely important. Even if you establish an agreeable atmosphere, you must still decide what questions to ask and how to measure and record the responses. The *STAR* approach has been successfully used by major companies and has proven to be an excellent way of matching candidates with the requirements of the job. The *STAR* approach is a behavior-based, experience-related interview process. It is built around the response of the individual to questions that are designed to identify specific activities in which the individual has been engaged in prior work. As a result a large part of the process is devoted to the preparation of the questions that need to be asked to best reveal the candidate's experience and readiness for the new position.

The interview process will be examined and applied in greater detail in the next section.

In this section we will delve into the development of specific questions as we evaluate applicants and apply the *STAR* approach.

An interview plan may start with the candidate's academic performance and lead to college activities if appropriate. It may then move on to summer jobs, early work experience, recent responsibilities, self assessments taken, plans for the future, outside activities and community service. Finally, a summary and then the reasons for leaving the prior job and/or seeking this job can conclude the interview.

Additional areas that are very specific to Christian organizations may be the person's Christian life experience, church involvement or doctrinal beliefs. Carefully worded questions with regard to lifestyle and social-ethical issues are critical if the person is being sought for a significant leadership role. As you go through the sequence of an applicant's life, the answers given will enlarge your knowledge of the four factors that affect his functioning; namely, *intelligence, skill/experience, personality* and *motivation*. Taking notes during the interview process is certainly an acceptable procedure but detailed note-taking can threaten the candidate and distracting the interviewer. A stream-lined rating sheet is therefore recommended, where notes can be jotted down on the four factors or other issues that surface.

Ending the Interview Session

Terminating the interview can be the trickiest chore of all. Because the applicant wants to look his best, he may linger, trying to improve his image. You must remain polite. No matter what your impression, ease the candidate out gracefully. Try to end with a summary of good qualities they have expressed. Provide them with the information they need regarding when, how and who will be making the decision.

It is very important to terminate an interview gracefully, for it represents the testimony and reputation of your organization. A rejected candidate should leave with as good an impression as the preferred candidate. By displaying a positive attitude toward your organization and the applicant, and by showing that you like and respect both, you will be well on your way to a successful conclusion of the interview process.

Interviewing is a delicate task – part science and part art. The science is having the proper design and behavior based questions. The art is in making the individual feel at ease and giving them the freedom to express themselves fully. Too often interviews end with neither the interviewer nor interviewee being clear as to what actually happened. A clear step-by-step procedure to the decision point should be evident to both parties.

Every company has, or should have, a pattern for employee selection and a format that is generally followed to ensure the right person is selected for the right position. Experience tells us that the problem of ill defined recruitment and interview procedures exists in far too many companies. However, it is a problem that can be remedied with the right people, in the right place, doing the right things when it comes to hiring people.

As an overview, if the following steps are in place and generally followed, the result will be a smoother and more successful outcome.

The first step in recruiting is the process of advertising. It is designed to solicit a number of qualified and interested people for the position that is available. The key to getting qualified candidates is to know what you are looking for and advertising the position clearly and in the right venues.

Step two is a method of screening the inquiries. Having certain employment criteria that state the minimum threshold requirements will be immensely helpful. This is the initial level at which names are removed from consideration.

The third major action is the in-depth data collection process which includes the behavioral interview. This step is critical to hiring success. At this point, the most promising candidates are thoroughly interviewed, implementing the job description and interview guide as important instruments to select "short list" candidates.

The fourth step is the decision making step. Here is where all the data is evaluated, the different reports from those who were involved in the interview procedure are compared and a final decision is made.

The fifth and final step is the actual job offer. Candidates who are not selected deserve a brief but honest communication about the decision that has been made and appreciation for taking part in the search process.

Pause and Reflect

Begin a planning process to look into ways your company can enrich and improve its prospective employee search process. Using the material in this section, start preparing interview questions, resume reviews and interview plans that will help you select the best prospects as future employees. Identify the people who will do the interviewing, train them and evaluate the procedures to ensure both professionalism and success.

The Behavioral Interview Principles

The behavioral-based approach of interviewing and hiring top candidates for your company begins with a full understanding of the overall concept. This approach has been in use for more than 40 years in major industries and has been effectively used in businesses of all types and sizes. It is based on the concept that successful past experience is the best predictor of future success in jobs requiring similar skill sets. When both employers and prospective employees understand the interview principles and techniques, quality matches are made in the hiring process.

It is common for interviewers to approach the interview as either an interrogation or a "get acquainted" session. The interviewer becomes a type of intimidator or else portrays themselves as a trusted friend. Traditional approaches include such questions as "Why do you want this job?", "What makes you think you are qualified for this position?", "What are your strengths?" or "what are your weaknesses?" The very general "tell me about yourself" is a common query.

Employment laws limit what an employer can and cannot ask during an interview. But apart from the legal restrictions and generally unprepared interviewers, better approaches are needed as traditional interview methods are not reliable as predictors of success for the employee in the new position. The behavioral-based technique has increased reliability from approximately 10% to greater than 50%. While this still is not a guarantee of future success, it is a considerable improvement over traditional methods.

Previous interview techniques employed hypothetical scenario questions that allowed the candidate to "create answers" to questions such as "What would you do if...?" or "How would you handle a situation like this?" Hypothetical questions permit the interviewee to answer without much verifiable accountability. The behavioral structured questions that call on the candidate to reveal past job-specific experiences tend to reveal authentic work related situations. In addition, as the candidate responds, follow-up questions can be asked to probe the thinking and decision making process of the candidate as the outcome of the behavior can be further explored.

In the final analysis, the interview process should be an effective tool in evaluating the candidate's readiness for the proposed position by comparing the responses with the types of experiences and situations the new position requires. When the interview guide is constructed, it will have categories related to the needs described in the position's description. Characteristics like learning capacity, critical thinking, adaptability, cooperation, independence and clarity in communication will be included. Often there are not a series of questions in the interview guide but rather a set of statements that lead the candidate to describe working situations or tasks. "Describe a situation where you had to…" or "Tell me about a time when you were asked to…" are statements that allow the candidate to tell, most often in story form, about situations or tasks they performed in the past, which could be very similar to ones faced in their new position. Experience has demonstrated that in these types of settings candidates will generally be very honest and either describe real situations or admit that they have not faced that issue before. Even that can be very revealing to the interviewer as to the integrity and forthrightness of the candidate.

The total interview process should be structured so as to have the candidate present completed tasks or situations. The interview really becomes a three-step procedure where a problem or task is described; the action taken by the candidate is presented; followed by the results or lack of achieved results. In the *STAR* interview process, the letters *S* and *T* stand for situation or task. The *A* stands for action taken and the *R* represents results. Every valid event must have all three parts or the event is incomplete and immeasurable. This will be examined further in the next chapter.

To summarize some of the key principles consider the following:

1. Use past behavior as a predictor of future behavior. While people grow over time and change (hopefully for the better), there is abundant evidence that we are significantly influenced by our past experiences.

2. Job related requirements (later referred to as job dimensions) need to be identified. These include mandatory characteristics such as knowledge, skills and personality expectations.

3. All interview elements must be organized into a comprehensive system. When completed, the interviewer must be able to draw all the information from everyone involved in the interview process into an intelligible recommendation.
4. The interviewer must apply effective interviewing skills and techniques. Thoroughness, objectivity and consideration for all candidates must be maintained by the interviewer.
5. The interview should be conducted professionally and respectfully. Time is a valuable commodity for both the interviewer and interviewee. Ethics and honesty should mark the process. Every interview should end successfully in terms of giving each candidate an honest and fair evaluation and leave them with an appreciation for the company that interviewed them.

Pause and Reflect

Personally commit to developing and using the behavior-based interview process, as you implement the STAR system. Devote enough time and personnel to establish it properly and prepare the appropriate documents and procedures. See the interview and hiring program as a valuable aspect of the business and the key to future company success.

Developing the Interview Guide

The interview guide is the interviewer's best friend. However, because it requires a great deal of time, thought and preparation, it is often neglected. Leaders who have been interviewing and hiring employees for some time may tend to rely on their past experience to conduct the interview rather than professionally preparing a guide that will help insure that the right questions are asked and the appropriate areas of the job are defined and explored. Unless this is done consistently, the ability to compare accurately one candidate and another for the same position is severely impaired.

Another failure is the tendency for leaders to seek applicants who are similar to them in personality, leadership style, likes and dislikes. This is a common tendency that will ultimately lead to an unbalanced leadership team, which although is strong in one area, exhibits weakness in other essential areas.

Five principles are important to remember when preparing an interview that will help you attract and select a balanced and competent team.

First, be sure the interview process is consistent from one candidate to the next. Some recruiters and interviewers let each interview take on a life of its own. When this happens it is very difficult, if not impossible, to make valid comparisons between candidates. The selection process becomes subjective instead of remaining objective. Making use of a common interview guide for all candidates will lessen this tendency.

The second principle is to explore each major area of inquiry with follow-up questions designed to define and explain the applicant's actions in resolving the situation they described. The interview will become a series of interrelated, work-centered stories that will help the interviewer better interpret how the applicant solved problems in previous job related experiences.

Principle three is to record as accurately as possible the applicant's responses to the behavioral questions on the prepared interview guide. The interviewer should take notes as unobtrusively as possible. Recording the interview may provide a more accurate record but is never recommended. Instead, develop the skill of listening to the applicants tell their stories while writing down sufficient notes to accurately record the experience.

The fourth principle deals with common courtesy. Although it need not be stated, it is very important. Maintain the candidate's dignity and self-esteem throughout the interview process. There have been cases, even in very fine companies, where the interviewer developed a dislike for a candidate and went on to demean the candidate during the interview with their tone of voice, improper questions, or a dismissive attitude. Interviewers represent their company at all times and must be gracious and remain objective.

Fifth, make sure the essential areas are covered, the right questions asked and the pace of the interview is appropriate and controlled. The interview needs to follow a planned schedule controlled by the interviewer. An interview can easily get off schedule when insufficient time is planned or when, because of the interviewer's lack of control, too much time is given to interesting but not vital areas of the candidate's experience.

Sample Questions:

To identify the difference between traditional, often theoretical questions and behavioral inquiries, consider the following:

Theoretical Questions	*Behavioral Questions*
What makes you think you can sell?	Tell me about the largest sale you made and how you did it.
Are you well organized?	Give me an example of a typical day for you, like last Monday. How did you plan it?
Describe your strengths and weaknesses.	How did your approach to finding customers differ from the approach used by others in your same type of job?
Have you ever ignored company policy?	Describe a time when you had to overlook a policy or procedure in order to complete a job.

Theoretical questions can often be answered with a simple "Yes" or "No" and therefore yield very little information. Behavioral questions elicit a longer and more descriptive response. In the behavioral interview setting, the objective is to determine how the applicant will respond to situations faced in the proposed job, based on actual past performance, not rationalistic projections. There is no guaranteed way of ascertaining the truth of their responses, no matter what interview system you use. However, experience has shown that people will typically tell you if they have not faced a similar situation, rather than fabricate a story to answer your question. When encouraged to tell stories about their work experiences, they normally go back to real life experiences rather than guess at the response you might be eliciting.

Another type of question to avoid is the leading question. This is a favorite of those whose experience in interviewing is limited. The differences between leading questions and behavioral questions are illustrated below:

Leading Questions	Behavioral Questions (non-leading)
I suppose you enjoyed working in sales, didn't you?	What did you enjoy most about working in sales?
I guess you left your job because you needed more money?	Why did you leave your previous job?
I suppose you agree that relocating your family was your biggest decision?	What was your biggest decision during the past year?

A good interviewer begins developing the interview guide with a checklist. It starts with the job description. Review and confirm the various dimensions; i.e., the requirements related to effective job performance. Sample job dimensions include such things as planning, organizing, problem solving, critical thinking, creativity, decision making and specific management skill like written and oral communication. The company needs to determine through its job analysis procedures which dimensions of the job are most necessary to perform the job with a high degree of success. This will depend, to a great extent, upon the complexity and organizational level of the position within the company.

For each job-specific dimension, there is a company-approved definition of what should be considered a foundational level of experience and knowledge. For example, for the dimension of creativity it might be, "The generation of and/or recognition of imaginative solutions in work-related situations." For the dimension of planning and organizing the definition might be, "Establishing a course of action for self and/or others to accomplish a specific goal including the proper assigning of appropriate personnel and resources." Once the specific definitions have been articulated the next step is the formation of the interview questions.

With the *STAR* approach in mind, the interviewer creates a series of questions for each target dimension. Each question should then be assigned an estimated time required to discuss it in appropriate length. The *STAR* approach is as follows:

Situation or Task	Describe in detail, a situation where you were expected to perform a certain responsibility or task related to your work. It can be from college, a previous job, or even volunteer experience.
Action	Describe the action you took, including what you did, in a step-by-step explanation of the event.
Results	Describe what happened. The outcome could be either positive or negative but the conclusion is important. Tell what you learned from the experience.

As the interview process nears conclusion, the interviewer reviews their notes and asks any additional questions to clarify the information received. He or she answers questions the candidate may have, explains the next step in the hiring process including the timetable for decision making and thanks the candidate for a productive interview. The interviewer then rates and reviews the responses given during the interview (in consultation with others who have been involved in the process) and makes a decision or recommendation regarding the candidate. Every candidate deserves a response, either verbally or written, from the interviewer. While specific reasons for the interviewer's decision need not be given, a professional attitude and courteous manner should be exemplified.

Pause and Reflect

*Circulate your newly developed **Interview Guide** among the top leaders in your company. Get their feedback and commitment to make the system work. Be sure that everyone involved in interviewing and hiring has ample opportunity for both input and training.*

Creating Behavioral Questions

One of the best ways to determine if you have created a good interview guide is through the use of behavioral questions. The behavioral questions that are asked should produce stories or descriptions of a person's behavior when carrying out certain job responsibilities. These types of questions avoid leading the applicant to predetermined answers or yes/no responses. They discourage theoretical responses to inquiries regarding working practices and experiences. Behavioral questions also are designed to avoid leading the applicant to the "right" answers as they are designed to reveal the applicant's actual past experience.

It is important to help the interviewee understand what a proper response is by explaining to them the *STAR* structure and providing them with an example or two to get them started. One of the very common errors is for the interviewee to start out correctly but not include all three major elements in their response. They may begin with a valid situation, a description of what they did to resolve the difficulty, but then project a theoretical or wishful solution that did not actually happen. This is called a "false star" because it is incomplete.

Try to avoid speculative questions as they tend to project future actions which are not verifiable, thus being of little value. Behavioral questions, on the other hand, ask the applicant to address experiences they have had, events or occasions where they performed certain tasks or duties, situations where their knowledge, competence, or even values were tested and examples from their working lives where lessons were learned and later applied to other work-related situations. Examples of such questions are as follows:

For Background Information:

1. What professional organizations do you belong to and what positions, if any, do you hold in these organizations?
2. As you have studied this job, could you give me an example from your hobbies or spare time activities that demonstrate a skill you believe would be important to this position?
3. Describe the process you went through that led to your decision to interview with us.
4. What were the circumstances in your life that led you to select your major field of study and/or employment?
5. What were/are your major responsibilities or duties in your present/previous jobs?

For Dimension-Related Information:

1. Initiative
   - How did you go about getting your previous job?
   - Tell me about a situation where you went beyond what was required in order to do your job.
   - Tell me about some new ideas or suggestions you gave to your boss about your job in the last six months.
2. Planning and Organizing
   - Provide examples of how you determine the top priorities in your work-week.
   - Describe a previous situation where you worked that required multiple and diverse tasks to be completed at the same time. Describe how you handled it. What were the results?
   - Describe your top work objective for this year. With whom have you shared it? What are you doing to reach your goal and where are you in the plan?
3. Professional Proficiency
   - Tell me about the most complex assignment or project you have had to complete. What was your role in the job and what happened?

- There are times when we are assigned a task that is beyond our capabilities. Describe a time when you had to request assistance on a project you could not handle on your own. What was the outcome?
- Have you received any work-related letters of commendation, awards or bonuses for outstanding performance? Explain.

4. Sales Ability
   - What was the best idea you ever sold to your boss? How did you sell it?
   - Describe your most disappointing experience in trying to get management support for an idea or proposal.
   - Tell me about an idea that you were able to sell to one of your colleagues. Describe how you got them to buy into your idea.

5. Judgment
   - In your present/previous job, what decision has taken you the longest time to determine? Why was this decision so difficult? Tell me about it.
   - In your present/previous job, what were the toughest decisions you had to make? Why were they difficult? What alternatives did you consider? What were the final outcomes?
   - Tell me about a decision you had to make that was not popular with other employees. How did you communicate it to the other workers? What was their response? How did you function as a leader in this situation?

To create perceptive behavior-based questions requires practice. Some samples that might help are as follows:

- Tell me about a time when you set and successfully achieved a work-related goal.
- Tell me about a time when you failed to meet one of your goals. What did you do as a result of that experience?
- Give me an example of when you had to carry out a policy with which you disagreed. What was the outcome?
- Describe a time when you had to dismiss a non-productive and/

or rebellious employee. How did you go about it and what was the final outcome?

- What has been the most difficult decision you have had to make on the job as a leader? What were the responses of colleagues and subordinates?
- Describe a successful course of action you took to correct an employee who disliked you. What did you do and how did you determine it came out well?
- Describe an unsuccessful course of action you took with an employee who disliked you. What were the final results in that situation?
- Describe the process you go through when deciding to hire an employee. How did you make the final decision? What was your follow-up procedure?
- Describe the process you go through when deciding to terminate an employee. How did you make the final decision? What was your follow-up procedure?
- Tell me about an individual that you invested your time in to help them grow as a person and better perform as an employee. How did they benefit from this?

Pause and Reflect

Take the lists of behavioral questions you have developed so far and ask your top leaders to review and revise the questions before using them. Realize that the question base will expand and change as time goes on. Keep it fresh and relevant to the work and processes in which you are actively engaged. Use these questions to discover the real potentials that your employee prospects have.

Conducting the Interview

Think back upon your own first experiences with job interviews. You will probably agree that most candidates come to job interviews with some degree of nervousness. After all, the person is venturing into new territory, meeting new people and will be asked a series of questions that are likely new to them. All of this can be frightening and unsettling. The experienced interviewer will do all they can to create an atmosphere that provides the candidate comfort and allows them to relax so their true personality emerges and realistic answers are given.

The very best interviews come from thorough preparation on the part of the interviewer. Companies that invest the time and appropriate resources in developing excellent interview procedures have a quality recruitment and selection process along with reaping the benefits of improved satisfaction from their employees. However, let me offer a word of caution. There are likely some people in your organization that should not be involved in the hiring process. Every organization seems to have employees who feel their job is to conduct an inquisition, rather than a productive interview process. Their tendency is to attempt to prove their superiority rather than find competent, qualified co-workers. Having been both an employee and an executive in several organizations, I have experienced both good and bad.

A number of tools will be needed if the interviewer is to conduct the interview in a professional manner. First, is the *job description* and identification of critical job dimensions as well as their definitions. This document needs to be carefully reviewed, especially if it has not been updated recently. Job responsibilities have a tendency to expand and contract around the strengths and weaknesses of the person in that position. Every new employee brings a different set of skills and abilities to the job. What was appropriate for the person who held that position previously may not be appropriate for the new employee in the same position.

The next order of business is the interview guide. This is the creation of a series of behavioral questions that are tied to the dimensions identified in the job description. Asking these important and probing questions will present the candidate the opportunity to share their experience and knowledge that has been gained in prior volunteer or employment opportunities. The answers to these questions will provide the interviewer with the best insights as to the potential success of the candidate in the proposed position. Again, the basic premise behind the behavioral based interview technique is that past successful experience is the best predictor of future success in similar situations.

Third is the interview process itself. Normally several people from within the company are given the opportunity to interview the candidate. Each specific primary area of qualification and aptitude is reviewed and examined using the *STAR* approach and behavior based questions.

The evaluation process follows the interview, as the results of the interview are shared with key leaders. Typically several people from within the company are given the opportunity to interview the candidate. Each specific interviewer is assigned to explore an area of the job description or candidate's personal life, with some overlapping of subjects to help build a multi-dimensional impression of the candidate. Each person who has taken part in the interview process then completes a form which helps them rate the responses of the candidate on the different items on the list.

The fifth and final step is to make a decision. The one responsible for making the final decision reviews all the reports, consults with the appropriate company leaders and the decision is made to hire or continue the search. If the answer is positive for the candidate, the candidate is informed of the decision and an offer is presented. At this time it is also appropriate to inform the other candidates in a proper and timely manner that the position has been filled.

A quality company recognizes the importance of making a good impression on everyone they meet. This is especially true when dealing with prospective employees. If a prospective employee leaves with an impression that the company is careless in its employee relationships, or even worse, does not treat people with respect and dignity, the message will spread throughout the community and industry. The people you did not select will be interviewed by other companies and their interaction with your company will quite possibly be discussed. Always strive to have the non-hired candidates leave feeling appreciated, respected, valuable and well treated. In my own experience, some candidates who were not hired returned years later with more maturity and better experiences. They became some of the best people I ever had the privilege of hiring.

The practical components of the interview process include the time, place and setting. Have a well-defined time limit, an interview location that offers privacy, comfort, freedom from interruption and a professional climate. Both the candidate and interviewer should have the appropriate job-related documents such as the public posting of the position, the job description, documentation describing the interview process, pertinent information concerning the company, salary range and benefits.

The interview will follow a guide that may include but not necessarily limited to academic background (from high school through higher education), jobs held while a student, other early work experiences, recent work experiences, self-assessment, future plans and expectations, outside interests and activities, community involvement, responses to the interview guide questions, summary and close of the interview. It will be followed by the evaluation and final recommendation. A well-prepared candidate will be familiar with the prospective employer, their mission, vision and core values statements, products and/or services, general clientele, position in their industry and the individuals in key leadership positions within the company. I have met many applicants who interviewed for a position knowing very little about the company to which they applied and consequently left a very poor impression as candidates. "Be prepared!" is not just a slogan for the Boy Scouts of America. It is a mandate for job applicants everywhere.

Pause and Reflect

Treat every prospective employee with dignity and courtesy. Even if you do not hire them, they can be ambassadors of good will for you if the interview experience enriches them and helps them better understand their strengths and potentials.

Special Terms and Sample Documents

Knowing the process is important but having the right forms to use is most helpful. This section provides a series of forms that an employer can use or, better still, modify to fit their specific needs. These are generic forms and can be changed to fit specific company formats and unique requirements.

Glossary of Terms

Target Selection	A behavioral approach to improving hiring decisions.
Dimensions	Character quality, skill, or personal attribute required by the job, as defined by the company. It is a description under which behavior can be reliably classified. It is what we want to know about the person relative to the target position.
Target Position	The job title for which we are interviewing candidates.
Data Integration	A meeting of those involved in the interviewing process to share information received about the candidate, reach an overall conclusion about the candidate and make a hiring decision.
Fluff	A hypothetical statement or assertion, not supported by behavior.
STAR	An acronym as a way for accounting for complete behavior. It consists of three parts: S = situation or T = task, A = action and R = results.
False STAR	Not a valid sequence of behavior. It could be a projection of feelings (vague), an anticipation (future oriented), or an ought-to-be (theoretical). The interviewee may think that they have described a complete behavioral episode but have not done so.
Job Analysis	The categorizing of the most common behaviors into groups based on similarity and placing a dimension name and definition on them.

Building the Interview Guide – A Sample

Writing Questions for Target Dimensions

With the *STAR* concept in mind, write two questions for each target dimension. Frame the first question in a positive light and the second one in a negative light.

Example:

Target Dimension: Creativity

Definition: Generates or recognizes imaginative solutions in work-related situations.

Questions:
1. Can you tell me about something you did where you had to create a new way of solving a problem or reaching a goal?
2. Can you tell me about a time when an established and tested method for solving a problem did not work?

Target Dimension

_____

Definition

_____

_____

Question #1

_____

_____

Question #2

_____

_____

Target Dimension
_____

Definition
_____

Question #1
_____
_____

Question #2
_____
_____

Sample Key Background Review
Prior jobs held
_____
_____

How did you obtain your former jobs?
_____
_____

Tell me about the major responsibilities or duties you have had in prior jobs.
_____
_____

What was the most satisfying accomplishment in your former position?
_____
_____

Could you provide an example from your hobbies or spare time activities that would demonstrate a skill or characteristic that might be important for this job?
_____
_____

Tell me about the most satisfying leadership experience you have had.

_____

_____

How did you decide that you wanted to interview with us?

_____

_____

Sample Dimension Interview Guide Sheet

Decision Making

Developing alternative courses of action, weighing the positive and negative elements for each course of action using logic and the factual information available at the time and choosing the best one to implement.

Tell me about the toughest decision you have had to make thus far in a work situation. How did you weigh the options available to you and what was the result?

Situation	Decision	Alternatives	Result

In your previous position, what decision did you consider for the longest period of time before making? Why was it difficult to reach a decision and how did you finally resolve it?

Decision	Situation (why difficult?)	Result

Describe the process you go through when you have to make a major decision that affects the life and/or work of other people. What decision have you made in the past that has given you the most satisfaction? Which one has given you the most grief?

Decision – positive   *Situation*   *Result*

_____

_____

Decision – negative   *Situation*   *Result*

_____

_____

Overall Dimension Rating

_____

Closing an Interview

People tend to best remember the things that happen first and last. How you begin with an applicant can set the tone for the session. How you end it will set the tone for their overall impression of your company. Here are some practical suggestions to ensure you have done your work well and are ready to conclude the interview.

1. At the end of the session ask a "buy-time" question.
   "As we conclude, take a few minutes to recall the things you have accomplished thus far in life. What is the most challenging thing you have faced and what is the most rewarding thing you have experienced? I'll give you a few moments to think about your answer."
2. Review your notes to be certain you have all the information you need before the candidate leaves.
3. Ask for an answer to the "buy-time" question.
4. Ask any additional questions for follow-up, or to complete missing information.
5. Answer any question the applicant has pertaining to the job.
6. Explain the next step in the selection process.
7. Thank the candidate for a helpful and productive interview and set a time when you will get back to them with a response.

Post Interview Instructions

1. Review the candidate information recorded on the *Key Background Review* section of your notes. Summarize the most important behavioral examples that relate to the position under consideration.
2. Review the information obtained in the *Interview Close*.
3. Read the behavioral information recorded after planned questions under each dimension and the notes on the responses of the candidate for each dimension.
4. Compare the recorded notes of any other interviewers and determine an overall dimensional rating according to the following scale:

   5 — Significantly above the criteria for successful job performance – Excellent

   4 — Generally exceeds criteria relative to quality of behavior expected – Good

   3 — Meets criteria in a relative manner – Acceptable

   2 — Not quite acceptable in meeting job requirements – Poor

   1 — Much less than expected and below entry expectations – Unacceptable

5. Share findings with your company leader, HR department and other involved leaders. Make a decision on the candidates.
6. Conclude the process by either offering the position to the best qualified applicant or continuing the search. Be sure to notify all involved (candidates and appropriate internal leaders) of the decision.

Summary

One of the most stressful and difficult tasks a leader is called upon to perform is the building of a quality workforce and maintaining that team. The search and interview processes are time consuming and expensive if done properly. A great deal of wisdom needs to be exercised in the process, a tremendous amount of patience and the repetition of the process has to be carried out as if each interview is a fresh and new experience. At the same time, realize that the candidates will widely differ in personality, skill, knowledge, experience, background, culture and values. All these facets must be considered and even then, the choice of the wrong person can be even more expensive and difficult for the company than no choice at all.

The best advice is not to hire in haste, for you will repent for a long time to come. Allow the responsibility the time and attention it deserves. Do not leave the hiring of your most important assets to "professionals," but invest yourself in it for the benefit of all concerned. Study it carefully and give it your best effort, for it will pay off in the long run.

Pause and Reflect

Having the right materials and presenting them in an attractive and professional manner will enhance your business image. Getting the right employees in the right places, doing the right things will make the business more profitable. You can be a benchmarking company for your entire industry and enhance your reputation by the quality of the people you attract as employees. Remember the modification of an old quotation: "A company is known by the people it keeps!"

Holding Out for the Best

When seeking leaders for your company or any organization where you have a passionate interest and vested concern, it is sometimes necessary to wait on the Lord for the right person. I firmly believe that "Whatever we do, in word or deed, we do it all for the Lord." Whether it is a board position we hold, a management role, or the enterprise we own, we have a duty to seek out and attempt to find the best possible people for our companies and organizations. Settling for less than that will always bring trouble.

If you are serious about being the kind of leader that seeks to honor God, you will confront the issue of how to be a successful business person while at the same time honoring the Lord Jesus Christ. Can there somehow be a way to think, act and live spiritually while making a living and leading others in the world of business? The answer is a resounding "Yes!" but it takes a committed godly leader to carry it out consistently.

In fact, the Bible indicates that God and man are both constantly searching for leaders in all walks of life. Leadership is expected in all types of organizations. In Christian enterprises as well as the business world, leaders are needed. The Bible addresses this subject and says that God is searching the hearts of people to find those who will honor and serve Him in all they do. Not just anyone, but someone who honors Him and applies His truth in daily decisions. It is also interesting that God is seeking individuals for leadership roles.

Consider these few biblical excerpts:

"The Lord sought for a man after his own heart." 1 Samuel 13:14

"I beheld, and lo, there was no man." Jeremiah 4:25

"Run ye to and fro through the streets of Jerusalem and see...if you can find a man...that executes judgment, that seeks truth: and I will pardon it." Jeremiah 5:1

"I sought for a man...that should...stand in the gap" Ezekiel 22:30

The Bible declares that God is seeking leaders and one leader, fully committed to the Lord and properly prepared, can and will make a significant difference in all types of organizations, be they profit or non-profit.

The overriding need in today's world is for leaders who are authentic, spiritual and sacrificial.

Authentic, because people love a leader who lives what he believes and honestly knows where he is going. That inspires confidence. They follow almost without question that man or woman who demonstrates wisdom and strength by adhering to what they believe.

Spiritual, because a leadership that is unspiritual and can be fully explained in terms of the natural, although ever so attractive and competent; will ultimately result in sterility as well as moral and spiritual bankruptcy.

Sacrificial, because they are committed to the One who gave Himself a sacrifice for the whole world and who left us the only perfect example of a spiritual leader.

There are many wonderful men and women in the Bible who were called to lead and did so with significant success, although far from perfection. In the Old Testament we have the examples of people like Moses, Joshua, Joseph, Gideon, Deborah, David and Nehemiah. In the New Testament names like Peter, Paul, Stephen, Mary and John filled key roles and made their marks as godly leaders. We could further go down through church history and find people who fulfilled the leadership qualifications of being authentic, spiritual and sacrificial. What we need, however, are leaders today who will "stand in the gap" and be all God wants them to be.

Spiritual leaders are not created by election or appointment, by men or by combinations of men. In the religious world leaders may be appointed by conferences or ecclesiastical bodies, but not created by these groups. It is important for every leader to realize that God is essential in making a godly leader and helping that leader to be successful. Simply holding a position of importance does not constitute a leader. Taking courses in leadership or resolving to become a leader will not do it. What is required is an individual who has experienced the grace of God in salvation, who commits their life to be and do what God requires and is willing to apply God's truth to their daily decisions and actions. Consistent, committed, biblically informed leaders are needed in all walks of life and all types of organizations. The way to achieve this is to prayerfully develop a plan that puts in place the right people, doing the right things, in the right way, with the right combination of talents, skills and supporting personnel.

In the realm of athletics, assigning a person the position of quarterback in football, pitcher in baseball, or goalie in soccer will not make that person either competent or successful. Competence and success in the athletic arena come from mental and physical preparation, a disciplined and practiced knowledge, experience in the game and the right blend of teammates fulfilling their assigned tasks to the best of their abilities. This winning combination is relevant in all enterprises.

Samuel Logan Brengle was one of the great leaders of the Salvation Army. He was a man of scholarship as well as spiritual power. He outlined the road to spiritual authenticity and leadership in the following words:

> It is not won by promotion, but by many prayers and tears. It is attained by confessions of sin, and most heart searching and humbling before God; by self-surrender, courageous sacrifice of every idol, a bold, deathless, uncompromising, and uncomplaining embracing of the cross, and by an eternal unfaltering looking unto Jesus crucified. It is not gained by seeking great things for ourselves, but rather, like Paul, by counting those things that are gained to us as lost for Christ. That is a great price, but it must be unflinchingly paid to him who would be not merely a nominal but a real spiritual leader of men, a leader whose power is recognized and felt in heaven, on earth and in hell.[14]

Natural and Spiritual Leadership

Leadership is influence; the ability of one person to influence others. One person can lead others only to the extent that he or she can influence them. This fact is supported by definitions of leadership by those who have themselves wielded great influence. British military leader Field Marshall Montgomery said: "Leadership is the capacity and will to rally men and women to a common purpose, and the character which inspires confidence." Former U.S. President Harry S. Truman observed: "A leader is a person who has the ability to get others to do what they don't want to do, and like it." And the former Chinese emperor, Li Hung Chang is believed to have said: "There are only three kinds of people in the world – those that are movable,

---

14 S.L. Brengle, *The Soul-Winner's Secret* (New York: Salvation Army Printing and Publishing House, 1920) pp. 36-37.

those that are immovable and those that move them." More recently, futurist Joel Barker defined a leader as "someone who will take you to a place you would not go on your own."

There are scores of leadership definitions. However, the essence of leadership is found in the person who is in a position of influence and who wisely and carefully communicates their vision, mission, core values and plans for success to others with integrity and consistency. Their life supports what their lips purport. Good and great leaders win through difficult times as well as good times. Oswald J. Sanders said it well when he wrote: "The crowd doesn't recognize a leader until he's gone. Then they build a monument to him with the stones they threw at him in life." Our legacy will always be in the people we have helped along the way and the honor we have brought to our God.

To be an effective spiritual leader means the blending of one's natural and spiritual qualities. It should be noted that even the natural qualities are not self-produced, but are God-given and therefore reach their highest effectiveness when employed for the glory of God. Personality is a prime factor in natural leadership. Spiritual leadership, however, and influencing others is not by the power of personality alone, but by a personality that is empowered by the Holy Spirit. Spiritual leadership is a matter of Holy Spirit-given power and that can never be self-generated. There is no such thing as a self-made spiritual leader. He or she is able to influence others spiritually only because the Spirit is able to work in and through them to a greater degree than in those he leads.

When searching for the next employee for your company, consider their past experiences, evaluate the degree of success they have had in similar types of positions or with the types of tasks that your available position requires. Expect and require complete answers that will give you an honest picture of how they work and what they have accomplished in the past. But do not neglect getting to know their inner heart when it comes to moral, ethical and spiritual issues. Carefully evaluate their answers to questions designed to reveal their prior choices and expressions of their value systems and spiritual experience. "As a man thinks in his heart, so is he," say God's Word. When we neglect what God has told us about selecting people for productive work we make a great mistake. When we prayerfully and carefully do what we should, His blessing will follow.

Once a person is hired the real work begins. Now the focus is on improving performance and preserving the progress. In the first year quarterly evaluations are important. After that meaningful annual appraisals should be done on all team members. Periodically, a 360 degree review will help keep the excellence process moving forward. It is far better and less expensive to keep good workers than to try and replace them. The old revised expression of "A company is known by the people it keeps," is valid. Be sure your personnel appraisal process is constantly reviewed and updated to include the best practices standards.

Pause and Reflect

Choose to be a quality leader with commitment to godly truth, biblical and ethical standards and a "best practices" mentality. Take time each week to evaluate your business one area at a time. Make a list of ways to enrich and improve your products, your services, your procedures and your profitability. God seeks your best and I believe that every earnest worker deserves a proper reward. Being a profitable enterprise that contributes to the good of the economy and humankind is our goal. Success is an attitude and an accomplishment. Be all that you can be for the glory of God and the good of those around you.

CHAPTER 6

LEADERSHIP AND COMMUNICATION

A survey was done of 100 top executives in America. They were asked a simple question: "If you had to repeat your college career, what would be you major course of study?" Interestingly, the survey revealed that over 90% indicated they would major in the field of communications!

Inherent in the very definition of leadership is the idea of communication. Being an effective leader requires you to be an effective communicator. Learning to read, write, speak and listen are not simply tools to get a person through school, but are essential components of leadership. To be able to communicate well is the mark of a good leader. It is the only way leaders convey their ideas, vision, directions and desires to others.

This is even more critical in today's world. Organizations are moving from a traditional top down authoritative model of leadership to one where teamwork, coaching and collegial forms of structures are preferred. As a result, companies and organizations of all types realize the need for leaders who value the input of their co-workers and associates. This approach requires enhanced communication and human relations skills. Modern leaders, regardless of the size of their companies, recognize the need for improved communications in their business for greater efficiency and increased profitability.

With the team leadership approach, organizations are realizing the need for leaders who act more like coaches as opposed to the long-established model of boss and manager. It has been discovered that being a team leader or a coaching type leader rather than a "boss" helps associates capitalize on their full potential. This new team approach builds self confidence, team accountability, self discipline and acceptance of the strengths and abilities of other team members. It requires leaders and managers to fill a coaching to those who are under their supervision. In order to be an effective leader and coach one needs to communicate to his or her people in a manner that brings results.

One example of this approach is clearly seen in the Disney Corporation where employees are known as actors rather than employees. This requires a more collegial and cooperative style of leadership instead of the more military or manufacturing style that has been popular in the past. It also requires a great deal more communicative and relational skills on the part of company leaders. In this model, workers are empowered and equipped to work more independently, with more authority while exercising greater intelligence and personal accountability than in previous generations. Whatever situations leaders find themselves in today, the leadership initiatives must begin with clear and effective communication.

Leadership has also been defined as an art; communicated through vision, words and actions. This view is critical to effective leadership as any strategic or directional initiative must begin with clear and effective communication.

Coaching in sports has unique yet significant parallels to leading in business. The responsibility of the coach is to instruct and teach his team to implement the goals and strategies of the game plan utilizing words and actions. In like manner the business leader performs a similar function as company goals, strategies and resources are assembled and allocated to accomplish the business plan.

The organizational structure of a company can benefit from this model of athletic coaching and we can draw several parallels between coaches and business leaders. Some of these parallels are as follows:

- Coaches expect commitment from players. Business leaders expect commitment from employees.
- Coaches expect to get results from the team and anticipate success and winning as they work to achieve the best performance possible. The same is true of business leaders and their associates.
- Coaches motivate and inspire players to their highest levels of performance and build trusting relationships. Today's wise business leader seeks to enrich and inspire their employees to reach their full potential.
- Coaches promote excellence and positive reinforcement among individual athletes and inspire and reward them appropriately. Business leaders also carefully measure the performance of their key players and treat them as most valuable assets, guiding their development so that nothing is left to chance.

Wise leaders know that the effective practice of communication principles in all endeavors builds trust between the leader and their team. It is the key to becoming an effective leader. Having the leader communicate the organizational vision, mission, culture and values on a regular basis to the entire company in verbal, visual and vivid practical ways builds trust and loyalty in the company. In today's world, this is not optional, it is essential.

How to Become an Effective Communicator

Effective communication is the very essence of effective leadership. Utilizing all the possible communication skills and methods available to you will make you a much more productive and appreciated leader. Being able to select and apply the appropriate communication method to the particular message to which you want your team members to respond, is key to being a productive and positive leader.

Legendary football coach Tom Landry defined leadership as "… getting someone to do what they don't want to do to achieve what they want to achieve." This describes one of the most important responsibilities a leader has: securing the cooperation of others in the shared enterprise. While others may puzzle over what leadership is, leaders recognize that that leadership is a dynamics communication process where one person is in the position of influencing others toward a particular objective. The leader's way of making the business purpose clear, the operational process understood and the end results realized is through a process of communication. This is where the follower's behavior is influenced and guided to the accomplishment of well-defined goals or targets. In the leader's toolbox communication skills are primary.

When referring to communication skills there are many more things to consider than words, sounds, listening, speaking, reading and writing abilities. These are foundational to our ability to act and interact with one another and understanding the significance of these elements can go a long way toward employing them properly. However, in today's world we have the addition of computers, smart phones, Kindles, iPods, iPads, gps systems and a host of other devices that people use regularly without really knowing technically how they work. Essentially these are communication devices and the more we understand their function, value and limitations, the better off we will be as communicators.

Top executives realize the critical importance of communication. A deficiency in this realm is particularly serious, as a primary function of leadership is the coordination of the work of others and the primary means of achieving coordination is effective communication. To coordinate the activities of individuals, a leader must interact with subordinates, superiors and peers. As a coordinator the leader must be able to direct the work of subordinates toward organizational goals. The leader must also be able to support the efforts of other managers by being able to convey to top management such suggestions as operational targets, personnel and policy changes and current issues needing resolution.

However, in today's world, an astute leader realizes that the work force is complex and that historical and generational changes have made for a diverse employee population. In his book *Coaching for Impact*; Dr. Jeffrey Magee charts five different generational perspectives and their specific characteristics.[15] The five generations are *Centurion, Baby Boomer, Gen X, Gen Y* and the *MTV/Mosaic* generations. In today's profit or non-profit organizations all of these are probably represented and each responds differently to leadership directions.

The *Centurion* generation comes from the World War II and Korean War era and they embrace a survival type mentality. Conservative in actions and desires, they value loyalty, security, hard work, understand frugality, are focused on the future and driven by principles and values.

The *Baby Boomer* generation is more flexible and given to valuing exceptions, varying nuances in situations, relativistic and grew up with a view of challenging norms, structure and the status quo. While being social experimenters in their youth, they have come to be more conservative in later life although remain generally materialistic in nature and recognition oriented.

The *Gen X* population grew up in a time of more affluence and as a result tends to be entitlement oriented. Their loyalty is contingent on how it benefits them; they are inclined toward disposable friendships and also lean toward the materialistic. As opposed to waiting for some future reward their focus is on "now."

Those in the *Gen Y* group tend towards technologically focused things and desire constant stimulation by sound or activity to hold their attention. Change is highly valued and action, even impulsive type action is strong and stimulated by a need to be different.

15 Jeffrey Magee, Ph.D., *Coaching for Impact* (Dallas: Brown Books, Inc., 2000) page 177.

A most recent generation could be called the *MTV/Mosaic* group and is very diverse, strong in personal relationships and somewhat more spiritually based. This spirituality, however, is a highly personal and generally not systematically organized or doctrinally grounded. They are more transient, divorce is more the norm, crisis is expected and anonymity is valued.

When all these groups hear a leader speak or read what has been written, they often hear or read very different things. An effective communicator recognizes the varied perspectives of those in the audience so that his message can be framed in a variety of forms to reach the greatest majority. There is a great deal of difference between hearing and understanding and every leader knows that creating understanding is their primary objective.

In the field of athletics, when an athletic coach instructs a player on how to play his/her position more effectively, the coach is communicating. It is through this communication process that they teach the players how to play the game most effectively. The same is true in both educational institutions and business coaching situations. The core of the educational and leadership experience is the teacher/student relationship, or the leader/follower relationship.

This dynamic is best personified by the famous remark of President James Garfield. He said that education meant sitting on a log with Mark Hopkins on one end and the student on the other. Garfield continued: "Give one a log hut, with only a simple bench, Mark Hopkins on one end and I on the other, and you may have all the buildings, apparatus and libraries without him." The relationship that exists between a leader and a follower, a teacher and a student, or an owner and an employee is the key to success in the human enterprise. Things like buildings, technical equipment or other resources may help, but without the vital relationship between leader and follower, the process fails.

As has been suggested, however, in the workplace of today we have multiple people with multiple perspectives. They all need to be guided to the same place on the same page, read the same language and be led to a common understanding of the facts being presented.

We all think we know what communication is. After all, we communicate all the time – when we arise in the morning, when we greet others on the job, when we begin the day reading mail or reports in the office, we are involved in communication. We continue to communicate by speaking to individuals, groups, or when we work on a report or prepare a presentation. But just how do we define communication? According to Webster, "Communication is a process by which information is exchanged between individuals through a common system of symbols, signs, or behavior." Since it sounds so simple, why do so many of us struggle with this subject? The answer can probably be found in an honest response to the following questions: Do others always understand you without the need for elaborate explanation? Or, have you ever had trouble in saying or writing exactly what you meant?

There are times when we all have difficulty in communicating with others. People call on the phone asking what our letters mean. A colleague gets upset over something we said which they took the wrong way. The reports we write get very little response and our directions go unheeded. We see that blank look on someone's face when we explain what we thought was an easy task. Sometimes we fail to understand others; sometimes they fail to understand us.

No matter how varied the activities or specialized the skills of a leader, in the final analysis, the job of every leader is communication. Essentially, the leader must get work done through other people and to accomplish this he or she must communicate with them effectively. This has been called the "X Factor"– that extra skill inherent in all activities – which means the difference between success and mediocrity for any leader.

"My job is mostly talking with people," said a company president when interviewed recently. His statement can be repeated by leaders up and down the line and at all levels of an organization. Calculations of the time the average leader spends in communicating by one means or another during the working day range between 50 - 90%. Thus communication is the management skill which the leader is most frequently called upon to exercise. It is perhaps the highest, most exacting, skill of management. Possibly it is also the most neglected one.

Compared to the texts in print on leadership and management, few books specifically address the development of communication skills. In spite of this scarcity, materials are available in a variety of forms – visual, verbal and audio – to help leaders advance their communication proficiency. Most individuals feel that since they learned how to write in school, wrote reports for teachers, have had to listen to parents, teachers and bosses for years, that they have the skills necessary for effective leadership. However, studies repeatedly show that communication is a neglected field of study for those aspiring to be leaders as well as those who are already in leadership positions. Leadership requires effectual communication and those skills can and should be improved.

Pause and Reflect

Think back over yesterday and recall how much time you spent in communication with others. To be more accurate in estimating, get someone to help you tomorrow keep an accurate record of how you spend your time. Time management experts suggest that every few months you should record in 15 minute blocks everything you do from waking in the morning until you go to sleep at night. Then, separate your activities into blocks of time and see where you really spend your time each day. This will also be an eye opener when it come to how much an in what way you communicate each day.

Common Stumbling Blocks

When a leader speaks, moderates a meeting, writes a memo or report, or settles in to read an article or report, that leader is engaged in a communication process. It has become so common to our daily experience that we seldom give any thought to how we do it, whether or not we do it efficiently or effectively, or how the message is being understood by our team.

A. S. Inglehart, former chairman of the board and president of General Foods, commenting on the communication process in industry and observed that we tend to be inept in communicating the ideas and information which create understanding among people who work in the enterprise. While this observation is a generalization, many leaders today would agree that time and money is often wasted when communication is neither clear nor relevant.

One reason for this occurrence is our tendency to mistake the form of communication for its substance. It is vital to know what you want to say first and then give consideration to the best means by which you can get the message out. While we may have made improvements regarding the techniques of getting the message, we have to some degree neglected the content of the message itself.

Secondly, we tend to oversimplify. We rely on employee newsletters, memoranda, public announcements or posted signs, rather than engage in personal interaction with employees on the job.

Third, leaders tend to talk too much and listen too little. We are in the age of information overload with directives, instructions and information on every subject under the sun and then wonder why all of our publications and speeches do not create clear communication.

Some leaders tend to look down on the subject of communication as a gimmick to be taken off the shelf and used as needed. Too few see it as the heart of the enterprise and the most important means we have of getting things done. Communication is the basis for understanding, for cooperation and for action. Whenever we are with other people we communicate in some manner and usually in more ways than one. In fact, when we consider communication in other contexts like the field of athletics, we see that athletes on a team learn to read their coach by the tone of voice, facial expression and physical movements. In the same manner employees come to read their leaders, even reading significance into silence or the words that are not said.

To most followers, the leader is the embodiment of the organization. As many have observed in the past, the leader casts a long shadow. Each word or action carries great weight although this fact may not be recognized or appreciated by many leaders. We need to recognize that it is not just the leader who communicates, but every single individual in the organization is also a communicator. In today's complex world of business, multiple languages with their accompanying cultural diversities further complicate the matter. For these and many more reasons, leaders must pay greater attention to the communication process.

Essentials of Good Communication

We usually think of communication as a single step of saying or writing something directed toward someone else. Actually, there are normally a number of levels through which this communication may go before it reaches the one for whom it is intended. For example, the leader has an idea of how to do something better. That idea is then passed on to another person who is assigned to carry it out. Finally, that person needs to take action and put the idea into practice. With any amount of real life experience, most people realize that instructions can mean quite different things to different people. What first seems like a simple process can become complex in just a few seconds. The simple expression, "Better clean up around here," can mean to one person that he should deposit the waste in the trash can, whereas to another it means stopping production for an hour while the entire floor is meticulously cleaned.

John Ralston, former coach of the Denver Broncos, was a coach who believed in persistent motivation and effective communication. As an accredited instructor for the *Dale Carnegie Institute* and a member of the *American Motivational Institute* and the *Success Motivation Institute*, he spoke often to different groups bringing encouragement and clear thinking from both his coaching and leadership life. Coach Ralston had a list of prime competitive ingredients the leader-coach needs to employ to make the players successful. These thoughts are applicable for all leaders and include:

1. The desire to get better. People must want to improve and succeed.
2. The need to be the best they can be. People must not settle for mediocrity.
3. The mastery of concentration. The mind tends to quit before the body.
4. The possession of intensity. Commitment to the goal is essential.
5. The demonstration of courage. The need to face the unexpected with determination.
6. The commitment to integrity and follow through in the face of adversity.

Another truth Ralston believed was that players (or as we think of our business, employees) must have a solid base of principles that are directed toward achievement, accomplishment and excellence if they are to be productive. To this end he developed a nine point set of commandments based on the word "intensity." With minor modifications the acronym is as follows:

I Intestinal fortitude – "American guts." The passion to follow through.

N Noise – Not words but actions – the sound you make when you exert effort.

T Training – Commit to be the best you can be by faithful preparation

E Energy – Proportionate effort to overcome obstacles faced

N Need – The proper place of pride in one's performance that inspires improvement and commitment

S Sacrifice – Give it your all or get out.

I Intelligence – Be smart but not a smart aleck.

T Thoroughness – Know your assignments and execute well.

Y You – The final key is the players' (employees') desire to be the best they can be.[16]

---

16 Jack Clary, *The Game-Makers* (Chicago: Follett Publishing Company, 1976) pp. 208-211.)

While a leader, manager, coach, or boss can work to establish the right rules, setting, opportunities and resources, it takes a solid commitment on the part of the "team" to make an organization, business or athletic team a success.

One final consideration before we look closer at motivation is the area of change. Communication is essential when changes occur in job assignments or when issuing promotions or new assignments to individuals. To be effective, a leader must learn to view things from both their own standpoint as well as from the standpoint of the individuals with which they are communicating. Understanding your "audience" is crucial not only for public speakers, but in any type of communication.

Pause and Reflect

Recall and evaluate one significant recent communication episode that took place during a normal day. It could have been the presentation of a new policy, procedure, the announcement of a new product or the acquiring of a new client. What were the questions that were asked by your subordinates, if any? How did you prepare to share your thoughts? Did you have a Q & A time and did it produce any new ideas or raise any new issues that needed to be considered? Was it a one-way communication or was it truly effective two-way communication?

Consider John Ralston's approach to communication using the word "intensity" as a guide. How many of his points were represented in your communication process? Wrap up your thoughts by making note of those things you need to spend time perfecting.

Motivating People

Leaders need to know when to tell, when to show, when to encourage and when to correct. These are not easy decisions to make, especially in today's business world with its hectic pace and multiplicity of tasks. However, the combination of showing coupled with telling has been a formula for success in many walks of life.

In the arena of professional sports, most successful coaches have mastered this formula. For example, Don Shula, the long time coach of the Miami Dolphins, declared it wasn't his job as the head coach to personally show players how to run, pass, block or tackle. There were specialists on the leadership team to do those things. His job was to set high standards of performance, pay attention to detail and demonstrate a pattern of hard work.

To reinforce his message he used to refer to the 1994-95 season when he was having difficulty with a calcium spur on his heel. He tried several ways to compensate for the problem and relieve the pain but did not want to take the time off during the season to correct the malady. He felt it would send the wrong message to his team. If he expected them to play in spite of pain, he had to demonstrate that he could do the same. However one day, as he was heading off the practice field he felt something pop and discovered he had ruptured his Achilles tendon. He missed one day of regular practice due to the operation – the first in his 25 years with the Dolphins – but was back on the field in a golf cart the next day. For Shula, example was a great motivator and he was one of the very best.

Motivation has been defined as "getting others to do what you want them to do, because they want to do it." Motivation has as a basic root the word "motive." That is what is inside a person that causes them to consider a concept, cause or action. Clarity is needed to get an idea across, but for the person to accept it and make it their own, the person must see the idea as something that they can and should do. The leader must not only *explain* what needs to be done, but *inspire* the followers to give it their best. Motivation is basic to teamwork.

It has been shown that open and honest communication generally results in improved morale and productivity. From multiple studies, it has become evident that improvement in communication depends less on investment in mass media than on the daily work relationship between leaders and followers. The leader must bridge the gap between upper level policy-making management and lower level operations and implementation of those policies and ideas. It may seem obvious to people that both leaders and followers benefit from increased stability and the accomplishment of objectives but for this to really take place, people must concretely see how they personally benefit and how they can contribute.

In order for this to happen, three things must be considered. The leader must provide the connections for the followers between: (1) the needs and policies of the organization, (2) the interests of the people in the organization, and (3) the leader's own purposes and goals. The last is very critical because whatever a leader does is colored by their own personal approach to and philosophy of their work. Knowing yourself, your motives, your abilities and your limitations is critical to effective leadership.

Communication is most complete where trust and confidence are present. A leader who is known for keeping promises, reporting facts honestly and listening sincerely will not have to fall back on a variety of gimmicks to maintain goodwill. In the long run, our followers are influenced not by what the leader says but by what the leader does.

Here are four maxims that are derived from this communication concept:

1. *Keep your promises!*
   The leader who invites requests for help or information and then disregards them proves that he or she is not interested in the followers' ideas.
2. *Give praise where it is earned!*
   Followers are quick to discount insincere flattery lavished everywhere in a conscious effort to create goodwill.
3. *Continuously communicate!*
   Communication must be continuous, not a sometime thing. Followers who feel the leader has their interest at heart will interpret constructively almost everything the leader does. If they feel the leader is against them, the leader will have trouble winning acceptance even for efforts exerted on the follower's behalf.

4. *Encourage two-way communication!*

While this theory is repetitively presented by leaders, in practice leaders tend to devote far more attention to telling, informing and commanding than they do to listening, asking and interpreting. Plus, even while impressively communicating, leaders may fail to tell workers what they want to know. To learn whether or not employees *really* get the message, the leader must encourage them to express their ideas and ask questions; then give careful consideration to any potential difficulty that they introduce. Problems may seem trivial at times; nevertheless, if they go unanswered they will constitute a barrier to understanding and to action. Here, as in all aspects of leadership, follow-through insures performance.

What counts in the final analysis is not what people are told, but what they understand. When leaders understand this concept of communication they can become effective leaders.

Pause and Reflect

What is your track record when it comes to getting others to cooperate and work with you to advance the goals and mission of the organization? When was the last time you focused on getting a complete understanding of what the team thinks about the direction and progress of the organization? How and how often do you do you solicit new ideas from your team?

The Communication Process

The words you choose to use as a leader are crucial to your effectiveness as a leader. So is your understanding of how the communication process works. Communication is not a one way street, it involves both give and take. It involves the giving and receiving of feedback. Clarity of thought, not just a multiplication of words, is the key. Words spoken or written, confirmed by action and support makes the difference. It also means leading by example. This can even include the recasting of the company's vision, purpose and goals for the intent is to keep the business and the work performed by the team members, on target.

Given a purpose for communicating and a response which is to be received, a leader intends to have their communication transmitted it high fidelity. Fidelity means that the communicator will generate a faithful reproduction of what they are sending forth. In technical language, a high fidelity encoder (sending device) is one that expresses the sound from the source perfectly. A high fidelity decoder (receiving device) is one that translates the message for the receiver with complete accuracy. In studying communication, we are interested in determining what increases the clarity of the message from sender to receiver.

Simplistic Model of Communication

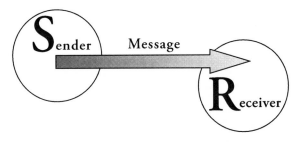

This diagram represents a simplistic model of communication we can call conversation. There is a sender, a receiver and a medium of exchange which is the voice of each person. However, communication is not that simple. If it were, there would be less confusion and a lot fewer mistakes made in today's world.

What follows is a more complete view of the communication process. Note the influence factors that affect us when we attempt to communicate. Note the type of process you go through as a leader when you begin to think about talking with an individual or a group and form your thoughts into words. Note also the possible interference factors that can corrupt your message. All in all, communication is a rather complex process.

A More Complete Model of Communication

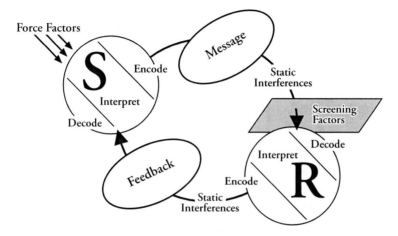

In a more complete model of communication you can see there are four major areas of consideration. There is the sender, the receiver, the message and feedback. There are also sub-factors for each of these four major ideas.

First, is the matter of the **sender**. The leader/sender must decide on the message to be sent. It should be clear and understandable to the receiver. This means that the symbols or words chosen to convey the message must be common to both sender and receiver. The sender encodes, or sends out the message. While that is in process, the sender is being affected by a number of influences, called "force factors" that may tend to either distort or clarify that message. These include issues as the attitude of the sender toward the receiver, the mental or physical condition of the sender, the location where the communication is taking place and a score of other factors.

Next is the **message** itself. Are the words loud and clear enough to be accurately heard? Are there other sound interferences in the environment that might distort the words? Has the correct setting been chosen to convey the message?

A third major element is the matter of the **receiver**. Every message is screened or filtered as it is received. This means there are competing ideas, possible misunderstood words, extraneous sounds and a host of other issues that can prevent a clear understanding of the message. As the receiver hears the words, does the receiver understand the meaning of those words? Are there distractions in the area that distort the message or does the receiver accurately decode the message?

Finally, is the matter of feedback. This is when the receiver has the opportunity to become a sender. They now encode, or send, a message. As with the sending of the message by the original sender, there is again the possibility of distortion due to extraneous sounds, plus the original sender (the leader) now becomes a receiver. Roles are reversed and this can be difficult for leaders who are comfortable with sending messages but not as good at listening for responses.

Communication is something we do every day and take for granted. Effective communication requires work and careful thought. Wise and effective leaders understand this and take extra pains to get it right. Once a message has been misinterpreted it is a complicated process to unscramble the mess. Wise is the leader who takes the time to get it right initially. Remember, communication is at the heart of leadership and effective communication enhances the image and effectiveness of leaders everywhere.

Creating Meaning for Others

Creating meaning in the mind of another is what communication is all about. To improve our ability to communicate we need to first understand that meaning and communication is a joint process between people. In addition, it is important to realize that meaning is composed of three elements (facts, feelings and intentions) and that facts are the least important of the three elements.

Individuals in leadership positions can seem to forget that communication is a cooperative process. Some communication fails because a leader only thinks about what they are going to say or write and forgets to view the message from the receiver's position. They send their messages believing that their workers or colleagues will clearly and accurately understand what they mean. The impression is that only the leader's meaning is important and that it can be poured into a receiver's mind like water into a glass. However, experience shows this is not the normal process. The receiver's experience is influenced strongly by their preferences, past experiences and personal tastes. What appeals to one person does not appeal to another. It is very similar to our food preferences. We like some things and reject others. When we review a menu we skip those things we do not like and search for more familiar and desirable items. In a similar manner, our differences in temperament and past experiences are filters through which messages are received and processed.

As mentioned earlier, there is no more powerful message than the one delivered by personal example. Differences melt away when one steps up to demonstrate a message by putting their reputation on the line to let others know what they really believe.

Jackie Robinson was the first African-American to play professional major league baseball. While breaking baseball's color barrier, he faced jeering crowds in every stadium in which he played. The story is told of how Robinson was playing second base one day at his home stadium in Brooklyn. In an attempt to field a ground ball, he misplayed it and committed and error. The home town fans began to ridicule him, heckling loudly. As he stood humiliated at second base, Dodger shortstop Pee Wee Reese came over and positioned himself next to him. Placing his arm around Jackie Robinson, he faced the crowd. The fans grew quiet and Robinson later said that Reese's arm around his shoulder saved his career.

One thing of which we can be sure is that when communication reaches another person, they will process it based on their meaning and understanding. We often hear things and instantly determine that the matter has no relevance for us and dismiss it immediately. To be sure that people will process what we say, we need to ask ourselves questions such as: What are they hearing and understanding? Are they concentrating on what is said, or are they resisting the communication? Are they being affected by some strong feelings? Does the person want to understand or are they just being polite?

One question to avoid is, "Do you understand what I am saying?" Few people will have the courage to say to their boss, "No, you were not very clear in what you said."

Communication is a social experience and the listener's reaction is vital to success. The nature of the receiver's reaction and response is determined not only by the words they hear but more importantly by what meaning they understand from those words. How the receiver defines and interprets the words is the vital link in effective communication. When we talk to others we are attempting to create a positive, productive, meaningful and harmonious relationship. Clarity and understanding are the twin goals of this process.

Emotions can be a serious impediment to effective communication. Emotions tend to distract one's attention and may also distort the meaning of that communication and make it useless – or worse. If you think back in your own experience, I am sure you can recall individuals who, though very smart and talented, were sometimes easily sidetracked because of their emotional attachments or perspectives. While we are all emotional creatures, learning when and where to allow emotions to have their place in our work is critical.

In addition to our emotions, past experiences are strong influencing factors in determining how a person interprets what is currently said. At any given time in a human relationship the character of the relationship may powerfully shape the meaning of a statement. Where confidence and harmony exist between people, communication is relatively easy and even the words used are comparatively unimportant. We "know" or "understand" what they are saying as a result of our history of interaction and positive relationships with them. We might even "not hear" negative things because we do not expect them to be said and so block them out even if spoken.

However, when people distrust or dislike one another, the scales are heavily weighted toward failure, no matter how carefully we choose our words. Emotions rule the day and even the most positive words are assigned a negative meaning. Like the maxim, "What we seek, we see," the communication equivalent is "What we expect to hear, we hear." We are selective listeners and a person's interpretation of a leader's words depends in large part upon the receiver's judgment as to the leader's total meaning as an individual as well as the specific meaning of the words in relation to him (i.e. the current intention they perceive toward them as receivers).

Creating meaning (communication) is a joint process between two or more people and is generally established in two ways. The first is the continuing history between people that is constantly being made better or worse as the relationship between them improves or deteriorates. This is an ever-lengthening chain of understanding and/or misunderstanding that is created by words and acts over time. The continuity of their experience places a special responsibility upon leaders. Wise leaders work at creating and maintaining positive relationships with their team to help insure effective communication over the long haul. Wise leaders ask themselves how they can make each communication to subordinates a constructive experience so that future communication between them will be easier and more productive.

The second is the type of setting or method one chooses to use in communication. Ordinarily it is either face-to-face or written communication. One key to success, only available in face-to-face communication events, is the ability to assess the listener's (or observer's) reaction; and if necessary, immediately help him to correct any misunderstanding. In written communication (unless subsequent verbal explanation is possible) one of the severest handicaps is the impossibility of testing a reaction on the spot. This is one reason why we are much more likely to succeed in transmitting an intended meaning when we talk with people face to face. This advantage is especially important in a new relationship or in an old one that has been impaired by dislike or distrust.

If we detect that our specific written purpose is not being understood, we can immediately try to clear the lines by informal conversation. Until this has been done there is no purpose in sending out more memos filled with extraneous words. In fact, additional words will do more harm than good. But when our relationship has been re-established, the specific meaning of what we want to say has a better chance of getting through. Shared meaning establishes a bridge of understanding, which facilitates future communication. This is something that leaders in the midst of pressing issues and hectic schedules are likely to forget.

In today's technologically oriented world, a word needs to be said about e-mail as a medium of communication. The use of technology and especially e-mail, has added yet another factor to the leader's communication concern. Being an instant medium as well as what communication specialists call a "cold" medium, it has introduced new potential dangers into the communication arena. "Less is more" and "quicker is not better," are two helpful sayings. Unless you will take the time to read your e-mail message from the receiver's perspective, you might make some serious blunders. Typing in only caps means "shouting" in e-mail language. Also, be sure to utilize the spell-check feature. Be careful of the "message line" and the "list of receivers" when sending the electronic message. It is easy to hit the "send" key but impossible to retrieve the message once sent. E-mail is a useful tool but be careful in terms of what you send as it leaves a permanent footprint.

Pause and Reflect

Reviewing the communication cycle may seem like an ordinary academic exercise. However, too many business leaders make assumptions about their abilities and practices in communicating that are simply inaccurate. It is a profitable use of time to periodically review the communication cycle to refresh one's self as to the important elements involved in proper communication technique. Take a few minutes to identify both your strong points and your weaker points in the communication process. Maximize your strong points by repetition as often as possible. Identify a weak point and work to overcome its negative impact upon your daily communications. Major on the strengths you have, but reduce the

weak points to where they no longer have a negative impact on your
performance. List both so you can check back and review progress
from time to time.

Making Meaning Meaningful

It should be obvious by now that the content of a message is only
part of its meaning. Even in the practical world of day-by-day work,
we constantly though not always consciously, deal with three components of meaning: facts, feelings and intentions or purposes. If we
were always aware of the function of each while we speak, write or
listen, there would be far fewer misunderstandings. What we now
want to address is what part does each play in meaning? And the
follow-up question of how do we handle them all more efficiently?

Objective Facts

Objective facts and the logical ideas that we have about them are
one element of meaning. These are expressed in statements which
we believe to be true and can be verified by testing, some accepted
standards or an experiment. However, problems can arise because
we do not select our words with special care. An alert leader watches
for signs of possible misunderstanding by other people and carefully
notes those who do not listen. Efficiency in each step of the communication process is important if communication is to succeed.
Leaders are especially obligated to be accurate and clear in facts but
they must also look and listen for signs of misunderstanding on the
part of others.

In factual communication the rules for efficiency are as follows:

1. **Be Precise**
    Have you ever had an idea that you thought was great but
    when verbalized it didn't sound nearly as good? It is like the
    predicament of the little girl who was admonished to think
    before she spoke. "But," she protested, "how can I tell what
    I think until I see what I say?" Words are certainly of help

to us in clarifying our thoughts, but in a relationship of
authority such as a leader has, he should not indulge in the
luxury of thinking out loud.

2. **Be Brief**

   Unnecessary words create extra opportunities for
   misunderstandings. They also subject us to the risk of being
   a bore. If a leader has the habit of wordiness, it will condition
   a listener to expect that many things that person says are not
   worth his attention.

3. **Choose Words with Care**

   Select words that will be easily understood by the listeners.
   Since the aim is to reach the mind of another person, it is
   essential to select words that fit well with their education,
   background and experience.

4. **Define Key Terms**

   In case of doubt (in a written statement, for example) or if
   misunderstanding is apparent (in face-to-face contact), it is a
   good practice to define key terms. In some situations the most
   useful method of definition is to give illustrative examples
   rather than define words logically.

5. **State Facts Concretely**

   If at all possible, state facts in terms of objective standards.
   Rather than saying something like "Boil each batch until it is
   good and thick," it is better to state the order as "Cook each
   batch for 15 minutes after the entire surface is covered with
   large bubbles."

6. **Avoid Abstractions**

   A concrete statement is easier to prove than a general statement.
   Besides, the precise meaning of an abstraction is very difficult
   to pin down. The slippery character of abstract words tends to
   make our thinking skid into areas of feeling and purpose.

Rules such as these are useful when helping us to communicate
objective facts. A second element in the process is feelings. Feelings
can give words a tricky twist.

Feelings

A feeling arises from and refers to subjective factors and experience. These are never exactly the same for any two individuals. We cannot measure and verify a sentiment as though it were an objective fact. Yet in dealing with people, we recognize that feelings are real and must be dealt with as such. It is sometimes more difficult to change feelings than to change external circumstances.

The most compelling feelings are usually our own. These are the only ones that we can approximately understand. It is also generally true that we appreciate our own feelings better than those of others. Sometimes they are the only ones we will acknowledge as being real and therefore are among our strongest feelings.

What we feel can have an effect all other elements of meaning. In any new situation it is natural to ask, "What does this mean to me?" From a moral viewpoint, a preoccupation with self is a negative thing and often is a subconscious process. It is only realistic to admit that we often have to deal with it both in others and ourselves.

Self feelings are often the most difficult with which to deal, but feelings of any kind raise problems with communication due to the subtlety in which they determine meaning. A communication difficulty familiar to all of us is the confusion between feelings and facts. While we may easily recognize this misunderstanding as it is manifested in others, we are typically blinded by the lack of differentiation between facts and feelings in our own minds. A "fact" is a unit of being, capable of bearing meaning. A "fact" is subject to interpretation in the light of other "facts" and our basic presuppositions. Because of this, most of us find it almost impossible to view our facts objectively, that is, to take them at face value.

The words "our facts" suggest the root of the difficulty. It is hard to be an objective reporter of *the facts*; it is much more natural to be interpreters and selectors of facts. What emerges becomes "our facts" and these supposed facts often show up in our opinions, our judgments and our purposes. Unfortunately however, another person's significant facts about the same situation may reach an entirely different conclusion. When this happens, it is difficult even for a disinterested third party to find an objective agreement that is wide enough to cover the whole story.

More often than we realize we "think" with our feelings. Self feelings, despite their intensity, can hinder our understanding and feelings of any kind can obstruct communication between people. They appear credible and seem more important than objective facts or principles. But only when feelings are appropriate to the total situation and are kept in their place can they be a constructive element of human relations. It is not difficult to recognize what feelings are appropriate; yet it is very difficult to get inappropriate feelings to a take a backseat where they belong.

As with any other job to be done however, a technique can be worked out. Here are five steps to help achieve this:

1. Realize the comparative unimportance of our feelings.
2. Appreciate the force of another person's feelings.
3. Acquire more facts: get the other person's side of the story.
4. Gain the attention of the other individual for additional feelings or facts which are pertinent to the situation.
5. Obtain agreement on principles.

Intention and Direction

Intention, or purpose, is a vital element in meaning. In trying to understand what is communicated to us by others, we are always searching for an underlying purpose. Often this is accompanied with suspicion as we use questions like: "What did he do that for?" "What is he really trying to find out?" or "Why did he say that?" Such remarks and any attempt to read between the lines are evidence of a search for purpose. We know this assigns meaning to the words and behavior of all rational people. Therefore we hunt for it as we attempt to evaluate what is not said and what is left undone.

Fortunately, however, our reliance on purpose works both ways. When we have confidence in a person's intentions toward us, we are willing to give them the benefit of every doubt, even when the specific words he uses seem unacceptable from someone else. Leadership can do its share in building mutual confidence by embracing the following key values:

1. Maintain open communication within the management structure.
2. Uphold obvious consistency between all management statements and actions.
3. Embrace honesty and sincerity in sharing information with workers.

When we have confidence in the stated purpose of an individual or group, it usually means that we rely on their good intentions in relation to both facts and feelings. Misunderstandings, between workers and leaders and even between organized groups, often find their origin in one or both of these meaning relationships.

Examples of this type of misunderstanding can be found in things such as: 1) doubt or disagreement as to the other person's ability to translate a sound purpose into fact, 2) subordinates losing confidence in their leaders if there is any doubt as to their sincerity, and 3) while some aims are short and others are longer in view, subordinates typically concentrate on short-term aims whereas leaders concentrate on long-term aims. Followers can benefit from a practice of lengthening their mental time span while leaders can profit from looking at things from the follower's point of view and developing short term plans, clearly communicated.

It is also important to realize that it is normal for leaders to focus on the benefits of a plan while subordinates focus on what it will cost them to carry it out. Leaders tend to inflate the benefits and discount the costs, while subordinates tend to discount the benefits and inflate the costs. A wise leader sees both sides of the picture and provides honest, candid and rational answers to the questions that are raised. This benefits all concerned.

In light of this, when a leader is called upon to present a plan of action, a new idea, or procedure to a group, there are four issues that should be reviewed by the leader before making the presentation:

1. **Does the plan make sense?**
   Do all participating parties understand the facts; have positive and proper emotional commitment to the project and its ultimate purpose? If the purpose relates well to key facts in the situation as a whole, there is a good likelihood for success.

2. **Has the purpose an ideal element?**
   A purpose has a strong appeal to others when it raises the expectations of the organization and when it emphasizes the "ought" rather than the "is."

3. **Does the purpose elicit satisfying feelings?**
   When our ideals are brought into play we recognize that our deepest feelings will come into action. This is one reason why organizations that have strong commitments and convictions are more likely to experience conflict than organizations that do not have strong convictions. Our ideals and convictions play a significant part in the communication and agreement process.

4. **Is the purpose timely?**
   The purpose may be realistic and laudable and may touch appropriate emotions; however, until the followers are convinced that it is also timely, they may shrug and say "So what?"

Pause and Reflect

How often do you use emotions in your communication process? Some leaders seem to be devoid of emotional communication whereas others seem to communicate everything with emotional tone and passion. Either excess is filled with problems. Emotionless expression is cold and unappealing. Emotional excess is wearying and confusing. Record a few upcoming presentations that you make and examine your balance of information and emotion. Have a trusted colleague evaluate with you the results.

Semantics in Communication

Words are often labels – verbal labels. Young children, for example, can communicate effectively for their needs and purposes by simply pointing to things. They point to food if they want to eat or point to toys if they want to play. Adults traveling in another country where the language is unfamiliar can often get along satisfactorily in the same manner. Such communication, however, is limited to tangible objects to which can be seen and pointed.

Many of our words are very much like pointing a finger. They simply represent the item that can be seen, touched, or otherwise clearly distinguished. Such words offer us a major advantage as they function as label words.

As we travel further away from such simple labels we become involved with words that refer to something intangible. Verbal communication now takes on a nuance or aspect of meaning that cannot be resolved by a simple unarguable, definition like pointing to an object. We come to a stage where our language has a meaning (value) to the speaker but often an entirely different meaning to the listener. This is where communication conflict begins.

For example, language that refers to specific objects or information to which you can point is called *extensional* by communication theorists. These are statements of fact in language that cannot go far astray such as "It rained 2.3 inches last night."

On the other hand, language regarding matters to which you cannot singularly point is said to be *intentional* ("The climate is wonderful"). Such expressions have different meanings to different listeners.

The story of the French painter Luis Quintanilla illustrates this distinction. One day a farmer was watching Quintanilla as he sat before his easel studying the canvas.

"You are resting, I see," the farmer observed.

"No, I am working," replied the artist.

Later in the day the farmer again passed Quintanilla as he was digging in his garden. "Now you are working," the farmer commented.

"Ah, no!" the artist answered. "Now I am resting from my work."

The message is clear. To the farmer digging is work and painting is restful. However, to the artist painting is his work and digging is a means of relaxation. Different people, observing the same event, can have different interpretations.

We interpret words in light of what they have meant to us in the past. We associate with each of them the very special meaning that we have learned and expect others to understand exactly what we intend to communicate. It should be obvious then, the more we can keep our communication on the *extensional* plane the less misunderstanding can exist. On this level, values are directly tied to the outside world and there is little room for personal interpretation. As we move to *intentional* language with its varying and personal "inside" values, we need to establish significant feedback loops to make certain that our communication is clear.

Communication Helps

Whenever we use tangible, objective words to convey our intent, we need to be confident that people clearly understand our meaning. Two important helps in this area are examples and visuals.

Examples provide clear, simple, easily recognizable verbal pictures of one or more specific manifestations of the words you are using. The leader must be sure the examples that are used fit the experience of the listeners and are reasonably free from elements that could distract from the intended significance.

The second help is the utilization of visuals or audio-visuals. Illustrations, diagrams or a more elaborate presentation can provide much needed explanation of concepts or ideas that would not be easily understood otherwise. This can be true of either written or spoken communications. Leaders must be careful, however, to recognize that some visuals are merely additional words or superfluous charts and do nothing to add explanation. Unless there are clarifying pictorial or diagrammatic forms to emphasize and amplify the concept, visuals may not be helpful.

Semantic Problems

Leaders realize that communication is hard work. The major necessities in effective communication will always be: 1) an awareness of the deficiencies of language and of the ever-present dangers of misunderstanding, 2) a determined effort toward effective communication, 3) a determination to avoid slanting language, and 4) a never-ending readiness to re-examine one's own assumptions.

Following is a list of eleven problem areas present in semantics and effective communication. Being aware of these pitfalls is the first step in being an effective leader-communicator.

1. *Similarities in experience or preparation may be deceiving.*
   Just because a leader went to the same college as another colleague does not mean that they both have the same understanding, attitudes or experience.
2. *Context and identical words.*
   Words are verbal symbols with different meanings in different contexts. What work is to a farmer and what work is to an artist are two different concepts.
3. *Context and individual differences.*
   Not only is the external context a factor but each person carries their own context with them. One word might arouse suspicion in one worker where it encourages productivity in another.
4. *The word is not the thing!*
   It pays to remember that a word is no more than a label. Like all symbols, words are useless and even destructive unless the speaker and hearer, writer and reader, use them to refer to the same things or the same values.
5. *Multi-valued words.*
   Many words have the characteristic of differing in value in different contexts. The word "job" is different from the perspective of the boss, the employee, the personnel manager or the payroll clerk.

6. *Meaning influenced by association.*
   We see words in light of our own context, need base, value base and level in the organization.

7. *Delay of reaction.*
   In general semantics advocates of the "delay of reaction" technique suggest that this is not exactly the same as counting to ten before starting to fight. That is simply a time factor. What this means is to not be controlled by your initial reaction. Learning to reflect and restate before responding is a critical skill to learn in the process of being an effective communicator.

8. *Talking back.*
   We are all more or less emotional; all of us are more or less susceptible to *signal* reaction. That is, in some situations certain words or attitudes can provoke us into non-rational responses. So can annoyances, especially when repeated or prolonged. This often happens with colleagues, superiors, family members, friends and subordinates. But if we want to really learn to understand each other, we must get past these crises and unite on friendlier terms in order to effectively communicate.

9. *Propaganda techniques.*
   Most discussions pertaining to communication take into consideration sincere types of communication. However, every leader knows that a great deal of speaking and writing in today's world is highly biased. That means that sometimes unconsciously, but more often deliberately, it is designed to convey or excite emotion. The language used is carefully designed to tell facts, not as they would appear to a calm, judicial expert, but as they appear to people passionately aroused about their side of a dispute. This can best be observed in political speeches. Particular words to some people are like waving a red flag at a bull. They excite signal reactions, violent and emotional. Many persons and too many leaders use such language (some intentionally) so that words may serve certain purposes. These purposes may be noble or ignoble but in either

case reliance on such techniques serves to impair future credibility on the part of the leader.

10. *Talking in absolutes.*

Unfortunately, many persons have a two-valued orientation. They see every issue in terms of absolute differences. A thing is good or bad; beautiful or ugly; black or white; up or down; yes or no; either, or. Everything is seen as one or another of two absolutes and nothing is seen as a matter of degree. Everything is either right or wrong. Either you are with us or against us. Teaching others that there are value differences and normally multiple alternatives to most problems is a leader's responsibility. The avoidance of absolutes, where they are appropriate, is also a danger.

11. *Use of subjective labels.*

Not only does the same word have different meanings to members of opposing groups but there is a very strong tendency to start calling something new names that suggest a speaker's attitude toward it. Words like "feather-bedding" and "scab" are subjective rather than descriptive. They tell nothing about an object or situation except how the speaker feels about it. The obvious answer to this problem is definition of terms. Many will not stop to consider definitions so the problem is not simple.

It is useful to think of words as a map and the subject under discussion as the actual geographic territory. The connection between words and their meaning then may be regarded as map-territory relationship. The map is not the real territory as the word is not the tangible item. The word symbols must bear a corresponding connection to the meaning that is like the relation of a reliable map to the territory it represents. The words must be understandable to others just as the map must be interpretable for anyone to follow it. But one must never confuse the map with the territory or the word with the object.

You cannot change the territory by changing the map. What you must be ready to do is change the map to make it fit the territory and not regard it as sacred or immutable. Like the charts and maps that discouraged navigators before Columbus, some assumptions upon which management policies and leadership styles are often based are like faulty maps. So in like terms, when your map and the other fellow's map both fit the territory – and not until then – you can have some hope of conversation about the same thing. And that surely is a basic necessity for worthwhile communication.

Pause and Reflect

How would you characterize your personal vocabulary? Do you have an extensive vocabulary base? Do you work at expanding and clarifying your vocabulary by doing various vocabulary exercises like the Readers Digest monthly word wealth? How much of your vocabulary is comprised of words that have a great deal of emotional overtone? Do you tend toward technical terms in daily work communication more than common words? Be sure that as a leader you know your "audience" and speak or write to them in terms they understand and appreciate.

Planning Your Communication

The essence of communication is to create understanding. People need to understand a communication in order to give it their best support. They need to accept an idea before they will do more than simply go through the motions. That is why communication is often put in the context of a salesman and his responsibilities. Communication must be sold; it must be directional and intentional. The word "sell" here means that you are communicating in a way that produces first understanding and then acceptance. The effective leader works at planning his or her communication, whether written or oral in form.

Here are five principles leaders should recognize and implement as they prepare to communicate their leadership directives:

1. **Know Your Purpose**

   As a communicator the first thing of which you should be clear is what you are actually trying to communicate. Know your:

   a. *Immediate objective.* What are you trying to accomplish: get action, change attitudes, acquire information, or something else?

   b. *Your long-range objectives.* Is your immediate objective compatible with the follower's objective? Is your message formulated so the listener will understand how it ties in with their interest?

   c. *Pertinent background and situations.* What made this communication necessary? What else is related here that should be considered?

2. **Know Your Audience**

   The more you know about the person or persons with which you are dialoguing, the better your chances for getting your message across. To make sure you are taking full advantage of all the information you already have, perform a mental check on the following items:

   a. *The best person to reach.* Does the individual or group you have in mind possess sufficient authority and responsibility to handle the communication?

   b. *The other person's background and experience.* Has this person been in similar situations? If so, how did he react? Does he have strong fixed attitudes toward this particular subject?

   c. *His personal values.* Do you know what this individual or group is trying most to achieve? What bearing could these goals have on understanding and cooperating with what you are trying to communicate?

   d. *The present state of affairs.* Has anything happened in the immediate past that may have affected the present mood so as to make them favorable or unfavorable toward your ideas?

e. *What the listener probably expects and hopes for from you.*
Clarify in your own mind exactly what authority and
responsibility the listener bears in relationship to you.
What do they expect to hear from you and what are they
likely to depend on you to provide? Are you likely to affect
motivation by what you say?

3. **Know Yourself**

   Most sales manuals do not include this point but it is essential
   because who you are and what you want are bound to be top
   questions in the mind of the listener as he judges your message.
   For this reason it is a good idea to examine the following:

   a. *Your fundamental goals.* Is what you are saying and what you
   are attempting to accomplish line up with your core values
   and ultimate goals?
   b. *What you stand to gain or lose from this communication.*
   While the listener is asking, "What's in it for me?" you need
   to also ask the same question. Some communicators indicate
   that it is a good idea to begin each communication with a
   frank statement about what you are personally going to gain
   from it, but this would need to be judged on a situation by
   situation basis.
   c. *Your communication habits.* Do you sometimes over or
   understate your case? Do you tend to talk too much, cut in
   on others, or assume too much knowledge on their part?

4. **Plan Your Approach**

   Consideration of the following issues is important:

   a. *Timing.* When is the receiver most likely to be a good
   listener? When will he be alert and relaxed?
   b. *Location.* The setting of the discussion or presentation will
   shape the receiver's mood or readiness to listen. Being on
   your turf or her turf will make a big difference.
   c. *Style.* While no effective leader will attempt anything
   artificial or deceptive, it is much better to start with the

positive rather than the negative. Presenting solutions and positive approaches is better than stating only the problems.

d. *Clarity.* Consider approaches that have illustrative devices to help clarify and emphasize the key points in your message. Pictures, diagrams or anything that helps the individual think more concretely is a positive communication step.

5. **Plan Your Follow-Up**

Following through on effective communication is the best way to provide a foundation for future effective communication. With that in mind, consider the following:

a. *Follow through promptly* with whatever action your communication suggested you would take. "Always follow through" is one of the oldest and most frequently overlooked maxims. Correct this by prompt follow-up.

b. *Plan then check every communication for its possible long-range effects.* No matter how well you communicate for today, you have failed if your message sets up roadblocks for tomorrow's communications.

c. *Try to foresee how your communication may influence others' communications.* Many a mix-up has been precipitated because a manager in Department A has spoken before considering if what he had to say would be compatible with the policy of Department B. Every communication concerns many people. Consider all who will be impacted by your communication and you will be a wise and more effective leader.

Test Your Communication *I.Q.*

Now it is time to check your own communication *I.Q.* Take the following communication *I.Q.* test and identify your strengths and weaknesses.

Check Points	Very Seldom	About ¼ of the time	About ½ of the time	About ¾ of the time	Almost always
I realize that what I see is an incomplete picture of what might be observed.					
I realize that what people say to me about a situation or person is a condensed version of what might be said.					
I realize that my interest and feelings may affect what I see, hear, or say.					
I use language in such a way as to specify the main parts of a message.					
When I speak I take into account the danger that some of my words may be misinterpreted.					
I am alert to non-verbal signs of misunderstanding and I adjust to such silent feedback by restating and improving.					
I show that I am glad to have listeners ask questions or restate my message.					
I avoid "allness" by quantifying and qualifying whenever possible.					
I use words showing degrees of difference when possible rather than two-value words.					
I use "you" and "we" in place of "I" wherever appropriate.					
Since the world of facts changes, I use words in their up-to-date meanings.					
I try to understand what a speaker means, in terms of his frame of reference, before I react to his statement.					
I am aware of whether I am stating facts, interpretive inferences, or value judgment inferences.					
I avoid using words that threaten the self-respect of the listener.					

Scoring: Give yourself 1 point for each *Very seldom* answer, 2 points for 1/4 *of the Time*, 3 points for 1/2 *of the Time*, 4 points for 3/4 *of the Time* and 5 points for *Almost Always*.

A score of 70 is perfect. (But do you put this understanding into practice?) A score below 42 indicates that you have a great need to improve your sending and receiving ability.

Pause and Reflect

Planning your communication is a time saving practice. It will not look that way at first but a few minutes taken to review, plan, outline and practice a verbal, visual, or written communication can save hours of correction and revision. Few leaders are able to prepare a presentation in a one draft manner. To get it right, to be professional and properly prepared, it takes dedicated time and the help of a number of close colleagues. Review the preparation points. Know your **purpose**, *know your* **audience**, *know* **yourself**, *plan your* **approach**, *plan your* **follow-up and review** *and you will be well on your way to a memorable and effective presentation.*

Time Out to Assess the Progress

We are now at the point where we need to consider the integration of your faith into your entire communication knowledge base. This involves thinking biblically, not just using biblical or theological term sprinkled through your speech so that you "sound religious."

Some leaders over the years who have had a personal relationship with Jesus Christ felt that they needed to play down the religious or faith side of their lives in order to reach their employees and friends. Sometimes they worked in government organizations that mandated they avoid any expressions of faith! What they would do is avoid any type of religious references in their presentations or writings and instead, sought to win folks by their life's work and testimony.

There have been other national and corporate leaders who have had a living personal faith in the Lord Jesus Christ and felt that they needed to be open and forthright about their faith. In so doing, they would reference biblical characters or passages in their public and private presentations as authority sources for their beliefs and actions. Some even placed such references in their official documents like mission and vision statements. This is more prevalent in Christian family owned businesses. In the experience of this author, publicly owned businesses avoid statements of religious faith as they are generally frowned upon in public even though I have heard leaders privately applaud this courage.

The question for the Christian business owner or Christian working in the private sector where there remains a degree of freedom to express your faith is this: *What is appropriate and effective in the marketplace when it comes to a leader acknowledging their dependence and confidence in God?* This is a matter that needs careful thought and prayerful consideration.

I have a friend who owns a business where the competition is open on Sunday. One reason is that it is supposed to be the most profitable day of the week in his industry. For many years he followed the crowd and his stores were also open on Sunday because it had the largest number of sales compared to the other six days in the week. He began to feel that this was a wrong practice because it violated the biblical commandment to work six days and set aside one day for worshipping the Lord. After much soul searching he decided to close his stores on Sunday. His reasons included giving all his employees a day to worship if they desired and to be faithful to what he believed was the teaching of Scripture. In shopping mall locations that by contract required him to be open, he modified his hours of operation to conform to their regulations and relocated to other locations when those contracts expired. His faith was demonstrated in the decisions he made and while some Christians and most non-Christians did not agree with his decision, he maintained his testimony and continues to be a very successful businessman.

Another corporation with which I am familiar, decided to openly declare in their mission statement that the corporation will not only continue to honor the values of its past and provide quality products but it will also strive to "operate in a way that will honor the Lord Jesus Christ." The CEO and Chairman of the Board, when speaking at numerous business gatherings across the country, has used that statement in various speeches and has been complimented for his courage and honesty. The same company, in its Philosophy of Business states in part, that it will "maintain and apply Christian principles in all our customer, employee and vendor relationships." Being a good steward of truth and having a commitment to quality in all aspects of a business venture is that which marks a business worthy of our participation in today's world of moral relativity and decline in the quality of products and services.

Just what a business should be and do in the midst of today's competitive environment and diverse religious and cultural climate is a critical choice point for today's leaders. The choices that are made in the areas of mission, vision, values, ethics and business philosophy are what will make the difference between a business that honors the Lord Jesus Christ and one that simply employees people for anticipated profit. Most appear to be satisfied with the latter. Those who seek the blessing of God upon their business and life seek the former.

Pause and Reflect

It is time to make some decisions regarding the purpose of communication, the style of communication and the content of communication you want to characterize your business. How open and forthright do you want to be regarding your Christian testimony as you present yourself and your business to the world around you? What steps will you put in place to ensure that all communication coming from your business will be timely, correct, complete and convey your message in an attractive and winsome manner?

Establish a procedure so that all you prepare, whether it be print, media, or personal presentations will be of the highest quality and clearest content possible. Surround yourself with honest, creative, courageous and talented people who above all have the highest marks in integrity and truthfulness and will make you a winner. The most important ingredient of all is character. Competency counts but character triumphs. To truly build winners seek to develop leaders around you who combine character, competency, commitment and courage, the four horsemen of effective leadership.

CHAPTER 7

BUILDING AN ORGANIZATION ON TRUST

ONE of the trends in today's corporate world is to define organizational culture and identify the style that characterizes current management and leadership. Each company, no matter how small or large, develops a culture and a style either by default or by design. The more successful enterprises understand that it is wiser and more profitable to develop by design than to just let things happen and deal with the aftermath. Developing a trust culture where leaders trust leaders, employees trust employees, leaders trust employees and employees trust leaders is part of their success. However, in a society that has been characterized as "dog eat dog," the concept of trust in the business world might be a difficult sell.

Character and truthfulness is at the core of the issue. When leaders act in a political, self-protective, defensive, self promoting and self aggrandizing ways, a competing and distrustful complement of workers develop. This chapter is designed to present the opposite view. It sets forth an agenda for building trust, productivity, cooperation and profit through a business that is committed to ethical behavior and activities.

Trust or Distrust: You Make the Choice

If you have spent any amount of time in the workplace you have likely confronted the issue of trust. Leaders who are insecure, inept in their skills, or uncomfortable with competent colleagues will generally mistrust anyone and everyone around them. They tend to continually look over their shoulders, always expecting someone to undermine their authority and challenge their position in the company. This atmosphere of fear and distrust poisons the culture, stifles the climate, drains creativity and retards growth.

What an incredible contrast it is to be in an organization that is grounded upon solid biblical and management principles, where employees are treated as assets and respected as individuals of worth; where trust and positive expectation is the norm and teamwork is universally embraced. This section is designed to help you better understand and practice leadership that maximizes trust and encourages your employees to become all God intends them to be as they work in an atmosphere of acceptance and honesty.

Booker T. Washington is reported to have said: "Few things help an individual more than to place responsibility upon him and to let him know that you trust him." Ralph Waldo Emerson echoed the same thought when he declared: "Trust men and they will be true to you; treat them greatly and they will show themselves great." But the observation I like best comes from D. L Moody. He commented: "Trust in yourself and you are doomed to disappointment; trust in money and you may have it taken from you; but trust in God and you will never be confounded in time or eternity." Trust is a spiritual exercise and those who know the Lord Jesus Christ in a personal way understand trust because they are trusting God for every breath and each step they take from here to eternity. It is a lifelong practice that also involves believing God's Word.

One practical name for this kind of company is a leadership

organization. It's not the amount of money you invest in the enterprise that makes the biggest difference. It is the type of leadership culture you develop and the confidence and security that comes along with it. If people believe they can trust you to provide honest and objective feedback regarding their work, they will become better workers and be the impact players all organizations seek. If a culture of trust permeates the business so that getting counsel and advice from other departments and divisions is expected to happen in a cooperative, rather than competitive manner, you have a leadership-oriented, trust-building organization. Mutual enrichment and corporate success are earmarks of a leadership organization.

Some years ago I visited a young Christian man who had become a successful leader in the building industry. I had just been introduced to the first of many books on the subject of building trust into your business culture. Wanting to encourage him, I enthusiastically shared with him a few thoughts on how this concept of trust in business can be a great model for Christians. Of course, trustworthiness is a way of life that the Bible presents for all Christians to follow. It is the ideal toward which we strive as we grow in grace and in the knowledge of God.

I was quite stunned by the young man's response. Not even waiting until I paused for breath, he interrupted me and launched his rebuttal. "People cannot be trusted," he said. "The only way to run a business is to make sure that your people are loyal and following the rules. That can only be done by close supervision of their work."

There may be truth to the adage that "you cannot expect what you do not inspect." When people know you are interested in what they do and how they do it, they tend to be more careful in their work. However, your attitude will affect how your employees view such an evaluative approach. If you communicate that you are not interested in what they do, that too sends a message. Without a meaningful plan and method of acquiring the proper information in an objective and non-threatening manner, an attempt to inspect all areas of your business can become an onerous task.

A company review will help determine the overall health of your organization. One way to begin is to take a single component that you believe is operating at an efficient level and start there. It will likely help you establish a base of criteria and expectation that you can later generalize to other areas of the operation. By beginning with the most productive and prosperous part of the business, you may also begin to communicate to the other areas of operation that you are not looking for problems but successes; not seeking errors but excellence.

The commitment to trust must be first demonstrated from the top down. Some years ago I was asked to conduct a series of seminars for a company that wanted to motivate its employees and improve morale. I suggested that it would be best first to conduct the seminar with the owners and top managers. Then, once some of the ideas for quality improvement had been discussed and accepted by the leaders and steps had been taken to demonstrate the leadership's commitment to continuous improvement and quality service, we could move down the organization and duplicate the seminar with the middle managers and other employees. At that point, everyone would be speaking the same language and understanding the same principles.

The owners and top managers felt that the plan was too involved and too lengthy and their desire was to see immediate improvement. As a result, the seminar was conducted in several repeat sessions with middle management and front line workers. There were a few positive comments, but most of the responses were cynical. "That might be the right way to do things, but it isn't the way things are done here," "Nobody in this company is willing to invest the kind of time, money and energy necessary to get those results" and "Upper management ought to be here taking this seminar " were typical of the comments. When employees believe that leadership does not practice what it preaches, only disillusionment and discontent will follow. When trust is absent and fear and anger take precedent, middle management and front line workers may even attempt to sabotage the very things that could be beneficial for them.

Pause and Reflect

Take stock of your company and its method of operational review. How is vital operational information gathered? How is objectivity maintained and used in the evaluative process? Is success measured in terms of output, profit, satisfied customers, company growth, or some combination of these elements?

Is there a common acceptance of what defines success is in the company? How are leaders rewarded and followers recognized? When managerial pronouncements are made, what is the most typical response from the workforce? How can you, as a leader, reinforce the idea of trust and productivity in the workplace?

Defining Trust in the Workplace

Trust means having the kind of relationship with others where you are open and honest and people believe you. Building trust means that you demonstrate your principles by your actions and following up with consistency. To proclaim that we put customers first, we respect each other, we are a team-oriented company, we operate by professional standards or we are a continuous improvement company is great – if the company performs that way on a daily basis. If the company does not demonstrate this in its overall operation, these positive claims can become a sarcastic epitaph.

Years ago, many of the major airlines created advertising slogans such as *We are ready when you are!* or *Fly the Friendly Skies.* These were well meaning and designed to highlight what the companies believed were their strengths. For many, however, the slogans were merely wishful thinking and the public took great delight in mocking them. As a leader, be both honest and careful when you create your slogans, mission, vision and statements of core values. Take special care to be sure you are describing the true situation and not merely expressing your dreams and hopes for the future.

Trust is a positive expectation of what other people will accomplish without the leader being in direct control or visibly monitoring the outcome. When a leader anticipates the best from the team, trust is evident. When a leader commits to supporting their team before the final evidence is in, trust is present. Trust depends a great deal on the investment the leader has made in developing positive relationships with various team members so there is a valid confidence in the expected outcomes of the tasks the team undertakes. While there are risks in any venture, the leader and the team share responsibility for making the enterprise successful. The key ingredients to building trust are reliance upon team members to use their best judgment, anticipation of positive results and expectation of follow-through to complete the project successfully without external oversight or excessive regulation and control.

The opposite of trust is fear. When situations begin to exhibit distrust, corrective actions of increased inspections, closer supervision and the addition of numerous meetings, memoranda and reports, the stage has been set for potential cost increases and competitive relationships. One fact that may surprise many leaders is that nearly every type of business has the capacity for mistrust and distrust. In the medical field, for example, you would expect to find trust and competency to be highly valued. Yet you can find evidence of suspicion and distrust between professionals like nurses and doctors or between maintenance personnel and administrators. My experience in higher education and with educational institutions reveal the same type of tension can exist. Faculty members can be suspicious of administrators; staff members can be critical and mistrusting of faculty members; and students may be suspicious of both staff and faculty. The biggest losers are the students who expect their teachers and administrators to be examples of moral and ethical leadership often end up disillusioned.

An atmosphere of distrust, rather than trust, is a ripe setting for negative attitudes and actions. Typical negative behaviors are seen when distrust is high. These include fear, fraud, excessive controls, political maneuverings, a high rate of personnel turnover, an attitude of uncertainty, increased competition and decreased cooperation; all leading to a loss of value, increased costs and decreased vision, energy and progress. A climate of trust is essential in order to lower costs, increase profitability, create harmony and empower the team. Building trust in your business must be a high priority.

Trust can be the glue that keeps things together in the business when trouble and tensions arise. Trust is more effective than loyalty as a force for productivity and creativity in the business. Leaders have reported that when workers buy into the company mission, vision, and core values with their hearts and not just their heads, the lasting positive accomplishments far exceed that of those motivated by loyalty. A major key to continuing this success is when the executive leadership supports the entire process through consistency and commitment. They demonstrate their support by providing the entire team with relevant and necessary information and encouraging confidence to complete their assignments successfully.

The question generally posed at this point is: "How does a leader maintain momentum and make sure that a trust culture becomes permanent in their business?" One way is to treat employees with respect and recognition for the contributions they bring to the company. Everyone wants to believe that their work has value, but not everyone can identify what those values are or what their leaders think those values are. A leader will build trust and trustworthiness into the fabric of their team by assigning team members meaningful work and reinforcing their dignity and showing respect for what they have accomplished.

Another major ingredient in the trust process is fairness in giving praise, rewards and recognitions. While this is important at all levels in the company, it becomes more important with those employees who have, or feel they have, little power or low status. Reinforce the trust relationship through some form of consistent and honest communication regarding their accomplishments. Let them know that you, as a leader, recognize their worth. This should not be done in a patronizing manner but with sincerity and consistency. In most cases an honest word of appreciation for their work will produce significant results. Since trust is built on integrity and consistency, make this type of recognition a regular practice by top leadership in all parts of your business.

Building a culture and atmosphere of trust takes time, focus, planning and the investment of capital over a period of time. Yet trust can be lost quickly over what may seem to be minor misunderstandings, uncontrolled mistakes or lack of attention to priorities and details. While trust is established slowly it takes even longer to rebuild once it has been broken. It is far better to work regularly at maintaining the trust base than to let it slip by through neglect. Where trust is lost, most times the leader can trace the problem to a specific event or action. The faster things are resolved, the easier it is to rebuild. The longer things are allowed to fester, the longer the rebuilding process will take and perhaps never be resolved.

Pause and Reflect

For additional insights on trust, read the following books:

> *Arky Ciancutti, M.D. and Thomas L. Steding, Ph.D. Built on Trust: Gaining Competitive Advantage in Any Organization. Chicago: Contemporary Books, 2000.*

> *Rita Cruise O'Brien, Trust: Releasing the Energy to Succeed. West Sussex, England: John Wiley & Sons Ltd., 2001.*

Make a list of things that your workforce will do without having to be told. Who takes the initiative to correct problems when they arise? What departments or divisions do you consider to be trustworthy in the company? Why are they outstanding? What transferable methods, principles, or practices are there to infuse the entire company with the same commitments and convictions?

Developing Trust in the Workplace

Trust is not a given in the workplace. It is a culture that must be carefully considered, wisely designed and patiently developed. Principal ingredients in the trust process are cooperation, confidence, participation, involvement and commitment.

Trust building is a patient, purposeful and planned process and has close parallels to fundraising. When a non-profit organization wants to develop a group of donors, the leader approaches it like building a customer base in a profit-making company. The language and terminology may differ but the process follows a similar pattern. The search for prospective donors is usually called the "suspect" phase. These are people who presently have no relationship to the organization but may become interested if the right approach is used and some personal connection can be made.

The next step is the "prospect" phase where steps are taken to test the suspect's interest level by providing pertinent information that applies to their areas of interest. If there are positive indicators at this point the prospect is usually asked to have some part in the organization by becoming a "contributor" to a project or participating in a program.

As the process continues, the person makes a financial investment in the organization as a result of seeing a need and identifying with how they can help. The skilled fundraiser seeks to enlarge the contributor's vision and increase their involvement through other avenues of service and giving opportunities. The contributor then becomes a "donor," or one who gives regularly, thus demonstrating their appreciation for and commitment to the mission, vision and value the organization brings to the community. As interest and commitment continue to grow, many donors have the privilege of becoming "investors," those who make the organization a part of their overall stewardship plan and support it generously and consistently.

This is not simply a money-seeking technique but rather a way of helping people support worthy causes in a good and godly manner. It could be considered a pastoral care process where one person helps another follow the biblical teaching on giving and helping others, if it is done according to biblical guidelines. It is a process that rests upon the foundation of building friendships. Relationships are formed with potential friends by serving or ministering to them in some way, meeting a need. Both friendship and cooperation are developed.

The old maxim declares, "If you minister to people, the money will follow." It is another way of saying, "God's work, done God's way, will receive God's supply." When you put money first you will get only what money can provide. If you put God first, you will get what God can provide. Let's apply this time-tested process to trust building. It should follow then, when you put trust first, you will get what trust can provide, or conversely, when you put distrust first, you will get what distrust can provide.

The first step in building trust is cooperation. The leader works to secure an agreement on what is likely a limited project, task or activity. This helps the team member feel that they are making a contribution to the overall welfare of the business. It begins to create the sense of initial investment.

The next step in building trust is confidence, or drawing the team member into a greater level of involvement. Now the team member has more knowledge and insight into the purpose and ethos of the business. It creates a deeper and more personal relationship with the company, but the team member still has no significant personal responsibility.

The third step is participation. The employee begins to take on limited assignments and accepts limited responsibility for success. Discovering the participants areas of interest, passion and commitment are essential for success.

The fourth step in building trust is involvement, where the person invests heart and mind into an assignment, exhibiting trust and a significantly greater level of contribution.

The final step in the trust process is commitment. The employee that invests in the company with both heart and mind feels an ownership and significance in the relationship. This relationship must be carefully nurtured and developed by the consistent actions of upper level management and top-level leadership. By this time, the investment in these employees has been significant and needs to be carefully nurtured.

What will help enrich and develop the team members, once they have reached the point of commitment? Mentally, it is the qualities of consistency, honesty, fairness, reliability and competency. Emotionally, it is open and accurate communication, compassion for others, mutual care and concern and a fair level of support throughout the relationship. Trust is like a beautiful hand blown glass decoration. It is carefully constructed, beautiful to behold, valuable to possess, but fragile and must be handled delicately. When cared for it is a delight to all who see it. When broken, it is a tragic picture.

Developing trust in a company requires a different way of thinking for many of us. It is actually a reversion to a very old concept taught by the Greek philosopher, Heraclitus, as a way of arriving at new ideas. In our traditional educational experience we have become accustomed to accepting the idea that someone else like a teacher or a manager has all the solutions. Our job, we believe, is to pay attention and learn what to think and do by listening to and watching others. Heraclitus stressed that by reviewing our own experiences, intuition and reflection we could discover these great ideas for ourselves.

While it has been said that "there is nothing new under the sun," most creative ideas come from individuals who know how to "scamper." *SCAMPER* is a simple acrostic to remind us that there are numerous ways to approach an issue and gain new perspectives. *SCAMPER* stands for *S*ubstitute, *C*ombine, *A*dapt or *A*dopt, *M*agnify or *M*inify, *P*ut to other use, *E*liminate and *R*everse. When you frame a problem in the form of a question and apply each of these simple but varied approaches, new ideas emerge. It works even better when you can engage several people in the process, for out of a large volume of ideas sometimes come the best solutions. When a company is fortunate enough to have a team who is prepared to face issues and problems in this manner, new and exciting ideas will surface. When team members are encouraged to contribute their ideas and perspectives to the success of the business, trust builds. Value and commitment follow.

Pause and Reflect

Write out your definition of trust as it applies to your organization. Next, list a number of ways that trust can be encouraged and developed in the leaders that report to you. Finally, lead your team in a discussion of how they can continue to spread the concept and develop trust in the people under them. Establish applicable goals and target dates for measuring your success in developing trust. Review with your top leaders the extent of your success and the methods needed to continue to process. Trust is more than having people say they agree with you and support you. It is best measured by a pattern of behavior that takes your company through the tough times as well as the good times.

The Trust Model

While most organizational systems are relatively easy to diagram, the trust model is not so much a structure as it is an attitude, a culture and a conviction. There are a number of paths, patterns or approaches to developing a culture of trust. Some of the identifying marks are common, whereas others may be unique to a specific industry or local business. Before we examine the common trust model characteristics it may be helpful to look at a few general identifying marks.

One trait readily recognizable in a trust-oriented company is the positive atmosphere throughout. Employees communicate openly with one another and with management; fear of reprisal or rebuke is absent. Leaders seek ways to encourage independent thinking and do not take disagreement as a sign of rebellion but as a sign of creativity. Leaders are self assured and have confidence in their team and their ability to think through and accomplish tasks.

The concept of "team" is not just a label but a reality in a culture of trust. Everyone is seen as contributing something to the success of the enterprise and recognized for their contribution. Rewards are not used as tools for motivating poor performers but as recognition of the sincere and measurable results produced by productive team members.

Let's examine what some consider trust to be. Dr. Duane C. Tway, Jr. in his 1993 dissertation, *A Construct of Trust*, defines trust as, "the state of readiness for unguarded interaction with someone." D. M. Rousseau and colleagues in *Not So Different After All: A Cross-Discipline View of Trust*,[17] offer this definition: "Trust is a psychological state comprising the intention to accept vulnerability based on positive expectations of the intentions or behavior of another."

Perhaps a further and simpler definition is offered by R. J. Lewicki and others in their 1998 article in *Academy of Management Review*, entitled *Trust or Distrust: New Relationships and Realities*.[18] They state that trust is "an individual's belief in, and willingness to act on the basis of words, actions, and decisions of another."

Whatever definition you select or develop, the essential elements in trust appear to include: 1) integrity, 2) respect, 3) consistency, 4) cooperation, 5) accountability, 6) fairness, 7) honesty and 8) open communication. These can become the core elements in the creation of any trust model.

1. *Integrity* – Trust is not a matter of communication technique or polished behavior, but of character. Integrity is a state of being whole, undivided in heart and soul. James writes that

---

17 *Academy of Management Review*, Briarcliff Manor, New York: Academy of Management, 1998, 23, pp. 293-404.

18 *Ibid., pp. 438-456.*

"a double minded (or divided) man is unstable in all his ways" (James 1:8). Integrity means pure, honest and upright.

2. *Respect* – When a leader creates a climate where the best interests of others are more important than his own interests, trust is nurtured. Creating growth and positive advancement opportunities for others demonstrates respect better than words can ever say.

3. *Consistency* – When followers can generally predict the leader's responses and actions to various situations, a trust level has been established. This is especially important when promises or commitments are made.

4. *Cooperation* – When a leader acts jointly with others, especially in difficult or uncomfortable circumstances, trust is created and nourished. It reinforces the "we" attitude, rather than the competitive "me vs. you" attitude so common in business.

5. *Accountability* – Taking responsibility for one's decisions and actions is becoming a lost art. Finger pointing and the "blame game" are more common than accountability. However, all healthy interpersonal relationships are ultimately based on personal responsibility and accountability. You cannot have a trust organization where personal accountability is not paramount.

6. *Fairness* – As with consistency, predictability and dependability are important ingredients in trust development. Here is where they are most clearly seen. Fairness means that truth will be sought, followed and valued. When leaders vacillate, change their mind frequently, or will not make a hard decision because it may not be popular, trust is destroyed.

7. *Honesty* – An essential element in integrity, honesty comes from the term honor and adds the practical element of truthfulness demonstrated in character and behavior. It means to be credible and free from fraud and deceit in word and deed. Trust cannot exist in an atmosphere that tolerates deceit.

8. *Open Communication* – A company that is grounded in truth and intent on building trust into the fiber of its culture seeks to listen, understand and respond with clarity, promptness and truthfulness to its various publics, from internal team members to external suppliers and customers. It demonstrates accountability and engenders confidence.

The trust model is a set of principles and core values that are practiced at all levels in the company, from the executive suite to the salesman on the street. Building a trust culture is a continuous process. It takes time to create but it can be destroyed overnight. It is fragile but incredibly valuable. Protect it, for once lost, it is harder to rebuild than almost anything else you possess.

Pause and Reflect

Post the eight items listed in this chapter where employees can observe them daily. Discuss with your key leaders ways in which these can help strengthen your business. Periodically add this discussion to your managerial meetings, seeking ways to strengthen the trust bonds within the company. Use these ideas in everyday presentations and reap the rewards of success.

Resolving Trust Issues

As we have found, building trust is a time-consuming process with great rewards. However, destroying trust can happen quickly and without warning. All that is required is a lapse of integrity or truthfulness. The best way to prevent such a disaster is to continually work at doing the right things, those that strengthen the trust factor and do not undermine the core values of the company. Pay attention to a solid mission and vision statement, maintain your core values as the guidelines for all you do and be truthful and transparent in communication with employees at all levels.

Start with truth as the norm in all communication so that employees believe your word is as good as gold. They will believe whatever they have seen you do over time, hopefully that you always seek to do right by them, by your customers and by the company as a whole. Trust is based on experience over a long period of time. Surveys such as those conducted by the Gallup organization indicate that when it comes to public trust, no one is trusted all of the time. For example, one survey group revealed that the United States military is trusted 64% of the time, police about 58% of the time and religious organizations about 57% of the time. Further, clergy, at the time were said to be trusted more than twice as much as journalists, who in turn were trusted twice as much as politicians! Trust is not something any leader can take for granted.

The larger the organization, the more difficult it can be to develop and maintain a culture of trust. Some have suggested that when the size of an organization exceeds fifty people, building trust becomes more challenging. One reason for this is that maintaining trust is a "high touch" issue. It relies heavily on consistent and regular contact between workers and leaders. When a larger group is divided into smaller segments, the trust factor is strengthened within the smaller groups but may be diminished in the larger organization unless there is a concerted effort to keep the communication lines open and honest.

Studies have shown that since nine out of ten people experience gossip and backbiting in the workplace, this has become the number one destroyer of trust. However, other violations of productive team functions are close behind. Broken promises, taking credit for another's work, micromanaging, violating confidentiality and "spinning" the truth will quickly break trust. Other behaviors that create distrust are excluding people from information and appropriate decision making processes, elevating one's own importance, and promoting and celebrating the accomplishments of underperformers.

Identifying problems is much easier than solving them. Take proactive steps to insulate yourself against potential problems. First, hire and promote people who fit well in a trust-based environment and who have an established track record of forming positive interpersonal relationships. Here is where an experienced-based interviewing and hiring process is most helpful.

Secondly, institute an employee enrichment program where leaders and followers are taught interpersonal relationship-building attitudes and skills.

Thirdly, follow up with a company-wide communication process that presents honest, timely and appropriate content to keep people well informed.

Four, create and promote the expectation that everyone will act with integrity and keep the commitments they make. This is especially important for those in leadership positions as they set the pace.

Five, resolve problems as they arise. When an employee consistently fails to perform yet appears to "get away with it," the entire enterprise suffers.

Six, listen to all employee concerns and take action when the facts and circumstances warrant it. Do not put off difficult decisions to a later date. Problems will only grow.

Seven, be a pacesetter. Never shirk from your responsibility nor act in a manner that would diminish your role as a leader and a coach. There is a fine line between being a leader and being a boss. Listen to the tale of the hunting dog named Leader. He was the best the guide ever had. Every hunter who used Leader always came back satisfied with all the game the law allowed. One day a repeat customer came and asked the guide for Leader and was told he was no longer available. Some previous hunter had ruined him! When the disappointed customer asked how that great hunting dog, Leader, was ruined, the guide answered, "The last man who used him forgot his name. Instead of calling him Leader, he called him Boss. Now all Leader does is sit around all day and bark orders!" The moral of the story is don't be a boss, be a leader!

Eight, hold people accountable for what they do. In my experience as a college teacher it was a disgrace to observe the way some professors would hold students strictly accountable for standards and deadlines on assignments, but they would be the worst offenders when it came to turning in their grades or reporting to administrators. The double standard will infect the entire company if permitted to exist in the workplace.

Nine, be sure to establish proper and reasonable boundaries. When you set expectations, follow through to be certain you are doing your part as a leader. Years ago, when I taught Sunday School to teenagers I required them to do homework each week on the lesson. My belief is that you cannot expect what you do not inspect. I found that most of the teens were eager for me to review their work. There is something in all of us that looks for recognition and approval when we try our best.

Finally, work at building a company that follows the "learning organization" model. If you want to insure that trust survives in your company, you must encourage people to be lifelong learners. In the learning organization, people seek to be growing, productive, adapting and appropriate risk-taking employees. Making mistakes is part of the fabric of life and from correcting those errors comes progress. Leaders learn to tolerate risks while maximizing the benefits and minimizing the costs. Encouraging and supporting team members as they engage in creative though risky ventures is building for the future.

Pause and Reflect

Develop a "trust policy" in cooperation with your top leadership team members. Share your ideas with all company employees from the owners through the regular workers. Support your policy with Scriptural references and post it in prominent places throughout the company. After a period of six months, survey your team members and gather examples of where trust is being demonstrated. Revise and refine as time goes on.

Building a Learning Organization

One of the best ways of developing a trust-oriented organization is to concentrate on building your company into a learning organization. This is not to be confused with an educational institution, for educational institutions are not necessarily learning organizations. Educational institutions are formed around the "teaching organization" model. In other words, they resemble top down business models like manufacturing companies more than cooperative and mutually supporting enterprises such as sports or research teams. The team-oriented organizational structures depend on each individual being a specialist but clearly recognize the value and contribution of all the players in the pursuit of success.

The concept of a learning organization was initiated with the publishing of Peter M. Senge's, *The Fifth Discipline: The Art and Practice of the Learning Organization*.[19] This 1990 discourse stressed the importance of interdisciplinary cooperation and integrative learning. It was followed up with *The Fifth Discipline Fieldbook: Strategies and Tools for Building a Learning Organization*, authored by Charlotte Roberts, Peter Senge, Rick Ross, Bryan Smith and Art Kleiner and the founding of Innovation Associates. Since that time, the concept or a learning organization has been explored in greater depth and numerous organizations have arisen to address various elements of it.

Because many individuals and groups have caught the wave of inspiration and excitement, there has been a continued expansion and enrichment of the concept so that today it is a major force in leadership thinking and organizational advancement. For those who realize that the informational age is passing and the age of relational and cooperative endeavors is upon us, the concept of the learning organization is central.

The core of ideas expressed in this approach is clearly supported

---

19 Peter M. Senge, *The Fifth Discipline: The Art and Practice of the Learning Organization* (New York: Currency Doubleday, 1990) 371 pp.

by biblical precepts. The Bible speaks often of a leader's work as a cooperative effort with God and others in accomplishing end results. As inspirational as it might be to have the good guys come to our rescue that is not the model that the Bible presents. Rather, the Bible teaches that we are "workers together with Him" in the pursuit of success and the contribution to progress. That implies a relationship of teamwork, collegiality and cooperation.

What does a learning organization look like? What are the major elements in constructing a learning type organization? First, as difficult as it might be to grasp, there really is no such thing as "a learning organization." It is not a structure or a form that one can diagram and replicate. It is more a series of operating principles and beliefs that are embraced and woven into the fabric of the organization. It has been described as 1) a culture based upon wonder, love, compassion and humility; 2) a group of values that magnify shared conversation and cooperative endeavors; and 3) a commitment to seeing the world and work as an integrated system of mutually important elements.[20] Because it cannot be simplified to a flow chart it, this concept might be ignored by some in leadership today who may need it the most.

It is so much easier to cling to the idea that there are great leaders and even heroes who will make everything right. The reality is that leadership requires insight into the nature of people in groups, commitment to core values and honest practices, clear and open communication, credible integrity, the reputation for giving credit to those who deserve it and taking the heat when things are difficult. The leader of a learning organization is a servant leader who engenders servant leadership in all who join with him. This leader is one who, with or without title, sees what needs to be done and does it without thought of promotion or reward. He builds into the lives of all those around him. He promotes the well being of both worker and company in a selfless manner.

---

20 For more information, see Sarita Chawla and John Renesch, *Learning Organizations: Developing Cultures for Tomorrow's Workplace* (Portland, Oregon: Productivity Press, 1995).

While the idea of bureaucratic leadership is foreign to today's "learning leader," so is the idea of leadership by committee. Leading by committees has become popular in many religious organizations and other non-profit organizations, just as bureaucratic leadership has become popular in most profit enterprises. Neither presents the profitable path for leaders described in the Scriptures. What then is the answer to this seemingly contradictory dilemma? Clearly understanding what it means to learn.

Learning is generally considered to be based on need. Learning to read, write, calculate numbers and process information are necessary skills to acquire. As a person grows they learn the skills needed for basic survival and later for significant purposes. Normally we think of learning as a *transactional* experience. There is a student who has incomplete knowledge or undeveloped skills and an experience "teacher" with advanced knowledge and skills. The teacher presents new ideas and methods for the student to learn and the student acquires that knowledge and practices the skill until it is useful and fulfills certain needs. This is quite appropriate for many types of basic learning such as buying, selling, or fundamental skill development. The problem is that this process is carried over into other areas of learning and is not a proper application.

A different type of learning is more appropriate to conceptual and foundational belief development. It is the *transformational* learning experience. This is not a neat, compact, and simple approach to learning, for it involves more than the acquisition of information or skills. Transformational learning becomes an internal examination of assumptions, basic criteria, multiple (and perhaps seemingly conflicting) facts and conceptual options, historical, cultural and physical evidences. It summarizes all this into a coherent, consistent pattern of thought.

When an organization brings together a team that is willing to learn together, support one another, disagree in appropriate ways, search for new and better ways of doing things, demonstrate respect for leadership and honor the mission, vision and core values of the group, you will have a learning organization with the potential for greatness. It will enrich and profitably serve its customers and community. It has a culture of commitment, caring and competency that is true to its convictions. It also represents trust in all its internal and external operations.

Pause and Reflect

For additional material on learning organizations and servant leadership read:

> *Sarita Chawley and John Renesch, editors, Learning Organizations: Developing Cultures for Tomorrow's Workplace. Portland, Oregon: Productivity Press, 1995.*

> *Peter Kline and Bernard Saunders, Ten Steps to a Learning Organization, Second Edition. Arlington, VA: Great Ocean Publishers, 1998.*

> *Larry C. Spears and Michele Lawrence, editors, Focus on Leadership: Servant Leadership for the Twenty-First Century. New York: John Wiley and Sons, Inc., 2002. (Focus particular attention to Part Two, Servant Leadership in the Workplace.)*

Consider your organization and determine where it resembles a learning organization with transformational learning taking place and where it is more like a bureaucratic organization with transactional learning as the main approach. What needs to be changed or altered? Where and with whom, can you start the process?

One Size Does Not Fit All

It may be tempting to seek solutions to problems by imitating what appears to work for others, but this is generally not the best solution. Over the years I have observed organizations that display a tendency to copy programs, structures or certain elements from others. Due to differences in personnel, cultural dynamics and philosophies that exist from one organization to another, this typically does not work. It is also the lazy leader's way of leading. In fact, some leaders have even copied the actual advertisements, documents, slogans and methods of others only to find themselves caught in an expensive retreat. Leaders need to lead and not follow, even when following appears to be so easy and attractive.

If duplicating the success of others is not the way to initiate change or resolve problems, what is a leader to do? The answer is to go back and review your company from top to bottom. Begin with your mission statement. Is your company faithfully adhering to it and allowing it to guide and direct your activities? Review your vision statement to see if you are still on target for purposes of future planning and evaluation. Examine your core values. Are they embraced by all employees and guiding the cultural development of your business? Is your planning process continual and being steered by the appropriate people? Have you recently examined and measured the effectiveness of your products and services in terms of use, profitability and relevance? Have you asked yourself, "What do we do better than anyone else and why are we better at it than others?"

Every organization is special and unique. The makeup of the personnel, the philosophy of operation, the individual cultures, the type and expertise of the leadership, the quality of the products and services all differ from one company to another or from one type of business to another. Every leader must decide and then focus on what niche they best fill and what future they sincerely desire. They must evaluate and select the team that is best suited to get them there. Their team needs a unified culture, commitment and competency to get the job done. A trust-based and trust-practicing company has the best possible chance of being successful in this endeavor.

You, as a leader, are charged with the responsibility of caring for the welfare of the business. Along with that is the correlated responsibility of doing the best for those whom God entrusts to your care as colleagues and workers. Your commitment to be honest, fair, kind and caring while leading your team to be productive, committed and full of integrity is an enormous undertaking. However, with the help of the Lord, by trusting Him on a daily basis, it can be done.

This brings us to the consideration of how should we evaluate and examine our business to be sure we are furnishing it the very best guidance and direction. The secret lies in having a purpose and plan for success and improvement and a schedule to follow to insure that it will be done.

Consider the family business as an example. First, review your management structure. Who are the top leaders in the business? How is each performing in their areas of responsibility? How were they selected and prepared for their positions? Do key managers have formal academic or outside practical business experience? What mechanisms are in place for helping top leaders enrich and advance their effectiveness? What policies are in place to bring family members into the business, or non-family leaders into prominent professional positions? By examining your top management leaders and identifying their contributions to the business you will better be able to identify needed skills, expertise and experience to take the business to the next level.

Next, review your governance structure. Do you have an independent board of directors who meet on a set schedule, report to the donors or stockholders and set policy? Do the auditors report to them directly all financial matters? Do they make succession plans and follow best practices guidelines for businesses in your category? How is the board organized? By what means and how often is the board evaluated? What methods of reporting to the board does your company use? Who chairs the board and how is objectivity maintained during and between board meetings? What do you consider a good balance between family members and outside board members for your business?

The official company documents that detail mission, vision, core values, operating philosophy and all handbooks, standards and operating documents need to be reviewed at least once a year. In a world where regulations, legal and business policies are subject to frequent change, attention must be given to keeping documents current.

Accurate financial records, productivity analysis, product and service viability all need to be reviewed on a quarterly basis under normal circumstances. In times of unusual stress or crisis it is critical that these be monitored more frequently. Emphasize a "no surprises" rule in your business. This can be accomplished through the old idea of "management by walking around." If an owner allows parts of the operation to go unobserved for too long and does not show interest or concern for the people and the processes in those areas, problems will arise. While workers do not desire to have the boss snoop around and continually look over their shoulder, they do respond well to the leader who knows who they are and what they contribute to the company. That can only be achieved by periodically spending time with all employees. How and when you do it is less important than the fact that you do it.

Leading and building trust into your company is a valuable and practical endeavor. It will pay large dividends in today's changing business climate. Be all that you can be and seek the help you need to stay successful.

Pause and Reflect

There are several fine organizations designed to provide helpful information and consultation for different types of corporate structures and family businesses. Invest in up-to-date literature regarding those areas where your company needs improvement. Consider contracting with a leadership coach to get you and your organization to a higher and more successful level of operation. Check with area colleges, universities, or successful businesses for people who might bring fresh and objective insights into your organization.

Helpful resources for family businesses include the following books:

Leon A. Danco, Inside the Family Business. Cleveland: Center for Family Business, 1982. Danco is the president of University

Services Institute and the founder of the Center for Family Business in Cleveland, Ohio.

Ivan Lansberg, Succeeding Generations: Realizing the Dream of Families in Business. Boston: Harvard Business Press, 1999.

Craig E. Aronoff and John L. Ward, Family Business Sourcebook. Detroit: Omnigrafics, Inc., 1991.

Bookstores and libraries are filled with current material that can enrich and give leaders the needed edge in today's business world. Be a student of your own organization or business and help it continue on the path of profit and success.

CHAPTER 8

WHERE DO I GO FROM HERE?

SOME books are meant to be inspirational, some informational and yet others are designed to be instructional. This book is intended to be a valued resource in your collection. It can be a volume that is visited repeatedly as various leadership and management situations arise. It seeks to provide help in all of three of these areas. There is inspiration in discovering how other leaders have thought and practiced the art of leadership. There is information about the different elements of leadership that every leader needs to not only know but remember in the hectic process of leading an enterprise. And finally, there are specific subjects that are presented instructionally with the express intent of describing in step-by-step order the process to follow that will enrich the organization.

You may want to use it as a textbook. Mark the pages repeatedly as you go through the material. Make the book your personalized study manual. Use it often as you lead and navigate the changing landscape of organizational dynamics. To lead effectively, leaders must constantly be growing in knowledge and understanding. Start, or add to your own collection of leadership illustrations, principles,

244 A Master Plan for Leaders

practices and guidelines. Strive to become a leadership oriented coach who desires, as part of their mission, to be a teacher. It has been shown in the past that no one in a learning situation learns more than the teacher. The teacher must first master the material, test it out in real life situations, conceptualize the principles that are involved and finally design a way to pass that material on to others. You are a leader. Commit to become the best that you can be for your good and the good of those you lead and have a great journey.

Before you set the book aside, or put it on the shelf for later recall, take a minute to review the material from a bird's eye view. By seeing the leadership role and responsibility from an overview perspective you can begin to better grasp the leader's privilege, process and procedure. First, put into your own words your definition of leadership. Give it your personal imprint by stating your personal belief regarding the ultimate source of your authority and power.

Next, provide a description of your mission, vision and core values statements. Begin to create plans for developing your potential. Do not rest on past accomplishments but be future oriented. Build stretch into your vision.

Third, make a commitment to correct and avoid those problems that have been known to derail leaders. Some of those "potholes" may not be a present problem nor have ever been a hindrance for you. However, there are likely a few that will plague you if you do not avoid the things that create them. Focus on the positive things you do and that cause you to be successful and steer clear of those things that can subtly destroy you.

Fourth, become a team builder. It has been said many times by many different leaders that a true leader has four outstanding qualities. They are character, competence, commitment and connections. While character is the key to the rest, it is the connections portion of that list that is vital here. A writer many years ago said, "You can't be human alone." He was stressing that as human beings, God has created us to interact with, learn from and serve each other while glorifying His name. A similar opinion can be said of leadership.

"You cannot lead alone!" We are dependent upon the help, expertise and cooperation of our team. The better they perform, the better you as a leader can perform. Form the right connections and focus on developing them to their highest potential and success is possible.

Connected with the idea of being a team builder is the key concept to recruit the very best team members you can. Remember that past experience in a position similar to the one being considered is the best predictor of success in the proposed job. Develop a company-wide policy and procedure that allows you to best match the person with the needed position. To make changes in personnel after getting someone established in a job is both expensive and difficult.

The sixth key to the process is communication. This actually permeates all the processes but needs our careful attention if we want to be a true leader of a great organization. It is no longer enough simply to be good. To be truly successful we must stretch for greatness. Making assignments, presenting those assignments to others, motivating people to complete them and a host of other functions, demand accurate communications. Leadership, which is influence, is the key to the leadership process. Become a master communicator by practicing the skill and art of effective communication.

The seventh step is to infuse your organization with a culture of trust which will build stability and productivity into your team. This final function will help make each and every day both positive and rewarding for both the leader and the followers. When people know they are valued, trusted and respected, they will generally do their best to continue to earn that value, trust and respect. Be creative in demonstrating this value within your organization with a variety of recognition and reward systems. Extra effort in this area can pay great dividends as you grow and prosper.

Finally, use the book as a guide for discussions in your management team. Pass it on to friends and leaders who you respect and will appreciate your help. Use parts of it in your newsletters and in-service training programs.

My passion over the years has been to help people discover their potential, understand what God desires for leaders and managers to be and do and pass on what I have learned along the way in my leadership journey. In this I hope a part of that mission has been accomplished. Be all that God wants and has gifted you to be by strengthening your relationship with the Jesus Christ every day.

SELECTED BIBLIOGRAPHY

THE following books were key resources consulted in the preparation of *A Master's Plan for Leaders*. These could be important and helpful to the reader for further information and growth in the field of leadership.

Allen, Louis A., *Management and Organization*. New York: McGraw-Hill Book Company, 1958.

Armerding, Hudson T., *The Heart of Godly Leadership*. Wheaton, IL: Crossway Books, 1992.

Arnoff, Craig E. and Ward, John, *Family Business Sourcebook*. Detroit: Omnigraphics, Inc., 1991.

Bennis, Warren G., *Changing Organizations*. New York: McGraw-Hill Book Company, 1966.

Chawla, Sarita and Renesch, John, *Learning Organizations: Developing Cultures for Tomorrow's Workplace*. Portland, Oregon: Productivity Press, 1995.

Ciancutti, Arky and Steding, Thomas L., *Built on Trust*. Chicago: Contemporary Books, Inc., 2001.

Clary, Jack, *The Gamemakers*. Chicago: Follett Publishing Company, 1976.

Collins, James and Porras, Jerry I., *Built to Last*. New York: HarperBusiness, 1994.

Collins, Jim, *Good to Great*. New York: HarperBusiness, 2001.

Danco, Leon A., *Inside the Family Business*. Cleveland: Center for Family Business, 1980.

Drucker, Peter, *Managing for Results*. New York: Harper & Row, Publishers, 1964.

Drucker, Peter, *Managing the Non-Profit Organization*. New York: Harper-Collins Publishers, 1992.

Hackman, Michael Z. and Johnson, Craig E., *Leadership: A Communication Perspective, 4th Edition*. Long Grove, IL: Waveland Press Inc., 2004.

Josephson, Michael and Holmes, Wes, editors, *The Power of Character: Prominent Americans Talk About Life, Family, Work, Values, and More*. New York: Jossey-Bass, 1998.

Kouzes, James M. and Posner, Barry Z., *The Leadership Challenge, 3rd edition*. San Francisco: Jossey-Bass, 2004.

Lansberg, Ivan, *Succeeding Generations: Reliving the Dream of Families in Business*. Boston: Harvard Business School Press, 1999.

Magee, Jeffrey, *Coaching for Impact*. Dallas: Brown Books, Inc., 2000.

O'Brien, Rita Cruise, *Trust: Releasing the Energy to Succeed*. New York: John Wiley & Sons, 2001.

Sanders, J. Oswald, *Spiritual Leadership*. Chicago: Moody Press, 1967.

Senge, Peter, *The Fifth Discipline: The Art and Practice of the Learning Organization*. New York: Doubleday/Currency, 1990.

Spears, Larry C. and Lawrence, Michele, editors, *Focus on Leadership: Servant Leadership for the Twenty First Century*. New York: John Wiley & Sons, Inc., 2002.

Wiersbe, Warren, *The Integrity Crisis*. Nashville: Oliver Nelson Books, 1988.

ABOUT THE AUTHOR

DR. GILBERT A. PETERSON (Ed.D., New York University) is a highly sought after authority on leadership and management issues. For more than 20 years he served as President and Chancellor of Lancaster Bible College (Lancaster, Pennsylvania). Additionally, he is past president of the Association of Biblical Higher Education and has served as the Director of the School of Christian Education at Trinity Evangelical Divinity School and Academic Dean at Philadelphia Biblical University.

Dr. Peterson has consulted extensively with leaders in corporate, non-profit and civic organizations. He has taught extensively on leadership and has authored or contributed to seven books relating to issues of leadership and Christian higher education. Gil and his wife Dolores reside in Lancaster, Pennsylvania.

Dr. Peterson continues to consult with selective organizations and can be contacted at gil@LeadersLifeandWork.com

CPSIA information can be obtained at www.ICGtesting.com
Printed in the USA
BVOW031911091011

273202BV00001B/11/P